Praise for *Check In:*

"Check In is a dynamic team habit that stretches us to pause momentarily and genuinely share important perspectives. It frees groups to innovate beyond routine 'Whack-a-mole' problem-solving methods. It routinely helps people know they are valued, that their input is wanted, and that their entire self is critical for success."

—James A. Laterza, Colonel (Retired, U.S. Army) Former commander/CEO, Landstuhl Regional Medical Center

"Dr. White is a change agent, disruptor, and soul stirrer. She cuts down to it and right to the heart of the matter. This is a real journey talking about real stuff that jumpstarts real transformation in all aspects of your real life. Some people are innately skilled, and some are masterfully trained. Krystal is both. Cliché, yes, but she has changed my life."

—Kevin L. Buford, Colonel, Board Certified Child, Adult, Addiction Psychiatrist and Coach

"This book teaches you a simple, but impressive positive communication strategy. Krystal's ability to lead groups always equips me to use powerful and practical tools. Dare to work with her and your skills will be sharpened. Ask her to lead A Big Share—it will break down barriers and build team cohesiveness."

—Royce Staley, MPA/HCA, RHIA, CCS Chief, Patient Administration, Defense Health Agency

CHECK IN

Krystal J. White, Ph.D.

Executive Shaman Publishing

Executive Shaman Publishing
www.theexecutiveshaman.com
krystal@theexecutiveshaman.com

Production by Stephanie Gunning Enterprises LLC
Illustrations by Eva Isabel Us
Cover design by Gus Yoo
Book Layout © Book Design Templates

Ordering Information:
Quantity sales. Special discounts are available on quantity purchases by corporations, associations, and others. For details, contact the publisher at the email address above.

Library of Congress Control Number 2020909035

Check In/Krystal J. White —1st ed.
ISBN 978-1-7335032-3-5 (paperback)

To you, the one who chooses to take in these words. To the one who is still a stranger, and to the one that reveals herself a friend. To the one I have chased, and the one I ran from. To the willing one, eager to be heard and listened to. To the hesitant one, unsure of what you really want to share, or what it really means. To you, who is relieved when it is not your turn; and to you, who is ready when it is.

Whoever you are, no matter how lonely or connected.

Wherever you are, no matter how lost or certain.

To you, who has arrived here. Now. At this start.

Trust that this—all of this—is again for you.

Contents

The Truth Is In There

eritas, Latin for "truth," guided the mindset of Roman civilization so powerfully that important tasks were marked with a "V" once they were completed. "V" conveyed to others one's truthful performance. Human intention often gets subsumed in the modalities and methods of communication. Quick penmanship, slow ink, or a preference for speedy communication soon transformed the emboldened "V" into a hasty check mark. It's literally shorthand to connotate truthful completion.

The image of the checkmark resonates deep within our spirit. Although some of us have forgotten it's power, the need for Veritas at the social level is palpable and promising.

Discovering the truth about people has never been more cumbersome than it is now. As a society, we have become so accustomed and reinforced to check things off, or check things out, that we fail to consciously check people in.

Social routines have been used since the beginning of civilization to mark our social statuses and arrivals. These processes are woven through all cultures and take numerous expressions. Take a moment now. Consider the last time you truly checked in.

Your answer probably involves exchanging updates with a colleague, friend, or family member. Perhaps you recently traveled, and it required personal identification and verification. You have checked in to obtain a driver's license, voter registration, marriage license or permission to provide a professional service. You have checked in to receive medical care, attend school, play on a team, join an organization, or exchange in commerce. Perhaps you have joined a religious institution or spiritual group, or been baptized, confirmed, or ordained in one; each requires a check in of some form.

You have checked in your entire life, whether you wanted to or not. The social routine is more essential and more prolific than we assume. Most of the ways we check in these days are automatic. The process has been short-handed to the degree that most of us fail to recognize and leverage its original intention and power. Rarely does it raise our social awareness or inspire personal truth telling.

Modern society prefers instant, individualistic gratification over slow, social progress. When it comes to our social routines, we often don't share our truth, or seek the truth of others. Yet, the human mind, body and spirit is hard-wired to assert an individual truth *and* sustain connectivity. We search for significance at a personal *and* a collective level.

We need social routines and processes that invite us to truthfully reflect about who we are and genuinely learn about people around us.

Veritas is on our minds and in our hearts, but we don't know where to start, when to listen, or how to efficiently express ourselves with the real people in our real lives.

The truth is inside of us.

This book outlines a single, simple process to meaningfully convey essential truths **together**. Learning to lead *Check In* will increase your capacity to relate to others with more authenticity, engagement, and compassion. These qualities must be cultivated to sustain trust and commitment in *all* your relationships.

Check In effectively improves ourselves for the benefit of others. With consistent use, it increases individual emotional intelligence and collective efficiency. Attention to social dynamics becomes sharper, better organized and more cohesive. A collaborative community is more likely to develop.

This book gives you a step-by-step routine that invites others to be more mindful, compassionate, and cohesive. After you have mastered leading *Check In*, you will find that it is the most efficient tool for changing the perspectives of others. It is a simple method for change management that does not rely on a cumbersome strategy or bureaucratic buy-in.

This tool is designed for today's contemporary thought leaders, entrepreneurs, and project managers. It also advances learning groups and teams who are committed to improving their collective performance. It works well for teachers and instructors aiming to instill social skills. Life or health coaches, mental health providers, therapists, and consultants can use it to optimize client responsiveness. It is beneficial for families that desire an easy routine to fosters honest, open, and fulfilling relationships. It is a great routine to consciously connect with your significant other, or the person you are dating.

Check In is paramount if we are to break free from the limitations of our current social habits and realized our shared potential. We need more people who show us how to honor our truths, serve others and, respect our planet at the same time. We need to be willing to *Check In*, **and** master leading it.

Who will choose to begin?

IT ALL STARTS WITH A

CHAPTER ONE

You *Can* Handle The Truth

The Ugly

Let's be honest about our modern-day social lives. Busyness, overstimulation, automation, pressure to produce and disconnection run rampant in our adult routines. We are saturated in experiences of being partially present, moderately engaged, or half-heartedly committed. We are *so* focused on getting things done, exchanging information, or making decisions, that it's hard to connect to ourselves, much harder to build resilient connections with others. We often are *so* dedicated on taking care of others, trying to please them or help them out, that we forget *who we really are and what we really stand for.*

"How was your day/weekend/vacation?"

"How are you doing?"

"What's going on?"

We hastily execute these greetings too often. Although they are polite, we seldom expect a genuine response back. Although most of us want to be better understood, we seldom provide a true answer.

 *Where do you consistently experience people who openly share with __and__ deeply listen to one another?*

The likelihood of you reporting that this experience occurred in a professional setting is low. When asked why they are leaving their organizations, talented employees often report that they "weren't listened to" by their peers and/or their leaders. Many people report that they started their small business in order to enjoy a more personal, people-oriented culture. These days, people want to "be the boss" in order to cultivate more fulfilling, caring connections with their clients and colleagues. Big businesses are facing the ugly truth that our professional lives often do not foster community.

Going a bit deeper, the likelihood that your response to the question above occurred in your current family or friendships is also low. Many of us don't know how to structure our interactions to be more emotionally honest and also kind. We desire reciprocity and autonomy but lack inspiring models that in our family of origin or early friendships. We know we need to be more vulnerable and more authentic, but we lack practical methods for relating this way. We often don't know how to respond when others are this way with us.

No wonder loneliness is prolific in many modern relationships. We don't have social expectations or habits to genuinely understand the real people in our real lives. *Check In* can change that.

The Bad

Most people want, seek and are given education to communicate better. Books, podcasts, and classes may be enjoyable and enlightening, but many of our insights don't translate into our real lives. Most of this information falls short when it comes to changing behavior. We talk the talk, but we don't walk the walk. There is so much information we seek or that is thrown at us these days. When we are thrown back into real life we often just don't have energy to implement or sustain our new ideas. We've all be there—we learn something new in our mind, but can't add one more new thing to try out in our already over-saturated real life schedule.

It can be a bit frustrating and dismaying to figure out where to start, even if you make the space for it.

If a person *does* know where to start or how to get the ball moving in the right direction, he will need to convince his colleagues, his partner, her boss, or her friends to "buy in" and try something new. Too often, he does not even try to influence change in his relationships. Or, he doesn't persist in sustaining the new dynamic. Sometimes, she may make time *and* influences others *and* persists, but does so in a way that is disconnected from those she leads. Soon, every one reverts back to life, partnership, family or business as usual.

Many of our well-intended ideals and well-informed improvement plans often prevent us from making *collective* progress This **lack of cohesive improvement feels bad.** It feels even more bad when we pretend that everything is fine/okay/good between us.

 *What do you need to be doing right now to experience amazing relationships?*

Many smart, kind people leak a lot of mental energy, dispel a lot of passion, and invest a lot of conversation in figuring out what it is essential. All this "Whack A Mole," or constant fixing and figuring out quickly trains our social attention on what's inadequate, confusing, scarce, or distant.

Inadequacy. Ambiguity. Scarcity. Separation.

I'm sure you can name an example where your work life or personal life has been weighed down by one of these mindsets. Any *one* of them easily influences us to overwork, burn ourselves out, and take a few other people down a negativity spiral with us. When all these four traits are present, our performance not only suffers, but our integrity does as well. Finding the truth within us and sharing the truth between us in this state is unlikely.

No wonder we frequently tune out! Tuning in and being engaged when these four things dominate our social lives is not sustainable. Eventually, we disengage, we complain, we withhold our thoughts and feelings, we defend our assets, or we stay in superficial terrain. This is business as usual.

Once we tune out, we don't know an easy way back into meaningful connection with others. This is particularly evident when we are at work, where we feel less responsibility to build emotional connections. We do not have easy tools to communicate prosocially as a team *or* in our personal relationships.

Check In achieves competence and confidence in the uncertain terrain of connecting with others. We *can* discern what we need to be doing together in a way that honors our relationships. We just need a method that we will *actually use.*

The Good

"I expect you to be here, here." This was the most compelling order I've ever heard a 4 star General give. I was speaking at a women's leadership symposium, and the audience was eager to hear how they could create a diverse and collaborative culture. The repetitive emphasis he made with the second "here" was impactful. It reminded me of roll call during the impressionable years of life, when roll call was an act of social significance. It provoked me to consider that we need constant reminders to be truthfully present together.

Many people don't consistently hold up to their end of the bargain on the decree of being "here, here." We all know people who say that they are "here for you" but really aren't. Often those that aren't "here, here" for us aren't bad, clueless or mean peers, partners, managers or leaders. They just haven't been exposed to or trained in a practice that invites them into deeper social presence.

Reminders help. They are insufficient when it comes to changing people's behaviors, however. (Just think of how many signs we have reminding people to engage in sanitary bathroom behaviors!) To observe outward changes, people need easy and practical routines to get "here, here." That's the role *Check In* plays.

At work, we often hear managers or leaders say it's important to "get to know people." Yet, how many people whom you worked for *really* knew you?

"Open-door" policies are common these days, but I am skeptical these strategies are effective at achieving their intended outcome. Has there been data suggesting that this specific team *needs* a leader to be available in this way? How many people are really utilizing it? Does it have the appearance of availability without reliably meeting the various psychological needs of its users? Is it there because that's "the right thing to do" or that's what the last leader did? Does the leader who institutes it need others to see her as being present? Is the team self-sufficient enough? Or does the leader micromanage every decision?

My experience has been that the most emotionally responsive leaders, the ones who truly **understand** others, aren't frequently accessed through open door policies. They are accessed through exceptionally emotionally reliable relationships, and they tend to demonstrate very clear boundaries regarding how available they are.

In our personal lives, we all have moments of being misunderstood and feeling like a stranger to those whom we want to understand us the most. We plan date nights, social outings, entertaining activities, and spend a significant amount of time together. And yet how often are we "Here, here" with one another? Accessible and portable technology, stimulating distractions, and competing preferences often impede a return on our investment. A shared, high quality presence is a rare experience.

Before I consistently used *Check In*, I thought I was "Here, here" with my people. Not just those in my work life, but also with my loved ones, my friends, and even my neighbors. I envisioned myself as the type of person that was easy to know and eager to understand others. I could have proved it with a plethora of facts: I have had a pen-pal for more than 20 years. I know what she's reading and what's growing in her garden. I am a psychologist. I've been educated, trained, and earned a living understanding with others. I love people. I am an extrovert! Of course, I *thought:* "I'm here with you, my people!"

Until I had a systemic routine for listening deeply, the truth is, I was kinda-sorta "Here, here." Half the time, I was *distracted* from the self-imposed to-do list in my head. The other half of the time, to be honest, I was spending most of my energy trying to prove to them, and to myself, that I was a worthy, good enough human being.

Check In changed the quality of my conversations, and the depth of my relationships. It slowed me down long enough to listen and engaged me up long enough to share with purpose.

The people who will unite others together now and in the future understand that they need practical, emotionally intelligent tools to tackle their own blindspots and address our society's shortcomings. They will implement new routines that help them live up to their own social standards. They will choose to be "Here, here" and help others around them to do the same.

I call these people leaders.

The Great

There are proven ways to get from good to great. For our purposes, the great result of *Check In* lies in how it brings people together without forcing compliance or conformity. The goal isn't to "get along." The goal is to discover the truth as we know it, at the time we are invited to share it. It moves us towards the elusive state of "being in it together" while maintaining our diversity.

Check In is a both an experience and a life skill that can reveal the best version of ourselves. I don't mean the "best" as in the edited or perfected version that we might idealize or project. (You'll find many typos in this book.) I mean the version of ourselves that flows from the truth inside of us, which is real and can be visible. Social experiences like these aren't necessarily nirvana-like and the group probably isn't singing "Kumbaya." Finding the truth within and sharing it is work.

It's exactly the type of work that our important relationships are worthy of.

What if the experience of being "Here, here" *and* together was more routine? People who consistently employ *Check In* can raise their capacity to be present, socially observant, caring, cohesive, and engaged. They will be more likely to sustain prosocial connection during the tough, awkward, or uncertain moments that are inherent in any essential relationship.

This is more important now than ever before, when many smart and caring people feel lost. Or they are lost and unaware of it!

One time I went to the wrong terminal to catch a flight from Europe to the United States. I made it all the way to the first automated security checkpoint without knowing I was in the wrong place. Several alarms went off. Still, I kept trying to go forward. Finally, a security person approached me and told me 1) **I wasn't where I thought I was**, 2) I wasn't in the right place, and 3) I wasn't where I needed to be. It was a loud and embarrassing situation. However, I was absolutely engaged and more committed to going in the right direction than I was five minutes earlier!

Insight should be provocative. Just like me, lost in that airport, most of us don't like alarms, and we absolutely value and need them from time to time. Similarly, some people may not initially like the structured process of *Check In*. Most of us get over that initial red flag quite quickly if we believe the tool, and others, serves a greater good.

Check In will help you and those you share it with to be "Here, here" *and* guide you all to where you intend to go. This book is your step-by-step guideline. It is organized by each of the 5Ws of the tool: why it works, how you use it, when you use it, where you use it and who you use it with. It gives you practical steps to discover your truth and listen to others so we can work and live better together.

Key Results

- ✓ Boosts Presence
- ✓ Raises Emotional Intelligence
- ✓ Decreases Distraction
- ✓ Improves Social Observation
- ✓ Deepens Relationships
- ✓ Enhances Engagement
- ✓ Improves Group Cohesion
- ✓ Fosters Genuine Recognition
- ✓ Accelerates Authenticity
- ✓ Cultivates Compassion

Values of Listenership

Using *Check In* consistently and competently will greatly advance our shared capacity to contribute to mindful, truthful, and reciprocal relationships. You should know the values that *Check In* endorses.

- ✓ *Every voice has space.* This means that every person present must contribute a response. This moves relationships beyond attempts to enforce equality and into practical ways to uphold fairness. During *Check In* every voice is valued and worthy--no matter the person's position, status, expertise, personality type, or interaction style. This is a rare occurrence in our modern day relationships and human systems, and yet we all long for it to be more routine.
- ✓ *Every voice must choose. Check In,* especially when routinely used and guided by an effective leader, stimulates respondents to answer deliberately. Why are you responding the way you are? What impact does it have?
- ✓ *Every voice is self-contained. Check In* prompts receivers to stay within themselves and not interrupt or intervene. It sets a clear precedent to allow the other person to give what he or she chooses to share. Acceptance, however temporary or superficial, is refreshing.

✓ *Every voice rests. Check In* motivates others to hear and listen, but it does not force or control them. Often, participants are "in their own heads" figuring out what they will say when they are called on. Sometimes people are distracted and not truly engaged. Those who are familiar with the tool get progressively better at being present with others. The structure prompts people to connect without having to talk.

If you're like many of us who want our relationships, professions, and communities to actively live and express these values, this is the essential tool you need to use right now.

How To Get What YOU Need from This Book

✓ Answer the questions and do the exercises. You'll be asked to *Check In* from time to time with yourself. Truthfully, do the exercises. You'll get better, faster when you slow down and reflect. Using a pen and physically writing out your responses is likely to stimulate more awareness. If you are one of the few whom *actually answers* the questions and complete the exercises, your results will be more visible to you, and more felt by others.

✓ Read *Check In* with a book club or in a group. This would be an inspiring skill for youth sports teams or family with adolescents to practice together. You are encouraged to read it with the team you manage, your community group, or a friend who is devoted to personal development. Read it with your business coach, business partner, mentor, accountability partner, executive team, or learning groups.

✓ Read it slowly. If you do read it quickly, go back and focus on re-reading a chapter a week in depth. During that week, only practice that chapter's specific skill. Ask for someone to observe your performance in that specific area to amplify your mastery of it.

✓ Try using *Check In* at least four times a week with others while learning it.

✓ Use one of the questions here for each week of an entire year. Don't go in the order they are presented in the book. Find the question that resonates with you the most at the time and lead with it.

✓ You will quickly learn the why, how, where, when and the who to lead a successful *Check In*. Skip to the How, Where and When chapters if you don't want to read some of the interesting scientific reasons why *Check In* works. The next chapter is not required for getting results, but the rest of them are!

CHAPTER TWO

Why *Check In* Works

R eading this chapter will help you understand why *Check In* improves our social relationships and optimizes group functioning. It explains the science behind each key result identified in Chapter One. For ease of reading, specific references are numbered and can be found in the End Notes.

Emotional Intelligence

The discipline of *Check In* is an accessible and useful tool that *efficiently* demonstrates *and* develops emotional intelligence.

In our current zeitgeist, recognition of the importance for emotional intelligence (EI) is quite strong. The World Economic Forum named high EI as one of the top ten job skills of 2020. Renowned books across multiple disciplines have been written on the subject, and diverse educational and training programs routinely involve it. You probably know someone who has invested in some type of "life" coach in the last five years. Health coaching, where patients become more aware of their mindset and behaviors, is also at an all-time high.

Research conducted from The Carnegie Institute of Technology concluded that approximately 85% of an individual's financial success came from skills associated with EI. Our technical competence in our professional craft drives 15% of our success.

Emotional Intelligence has four main components: 1) Self Awareness 2) Self Management 3) Social Awareness 4) Relationship Management[1]. People who already have high EI will naturally appreciate *Check In*. For those that want to improve their EI, becoming competent at using the tool will raise their abilities in each of EI's main four main components. Both groups will appreciate the structure provided here and find the list of questions valuable. Since EI competence involves people, and *people are dynamic and always changing,* no matter how "high" your EI is, you need to constantly "check in" with it and nurture it.

As a leadership psychologist specializing in prosocial performance, I frequently guide others to improve their EI. One objective is to improve "ego management." I specifically use the term "ego." It acknowledges that we all have preferred ways we see ourselves, and interpret experiences. Each of us have a unique way of operating, which is similar to our mind's own individualized software program. It can either work for us, or against us. It can either work for others, or against others. Like technology, our egos frequently need to be re-booted, checked for viruses and updated or swapped altogether.

Ego management is an essential requirement to sustain healthy relationships and gain social influence. It is critical to understand ourselves at deeper levels beyond that of our preferences, our plans, our worries and our impressions. We can't manage, much less lead, something that is essential if we only understand it superficially.

We want the instant gratification of behavior change, without really putting much effort to master our own thoughts and feelings In this world, we educate and train people to understand external objects more than their own internal landscapes.. It is easier to examine things we can visually perceive than those we internally notice. None of us walk around with a mirror in front of us, and many of us actively work to put on a different "face" to perform certain roles. It often is socially accepted and even advised for us to be nice, look good, and pretend not to "know" some hard to face truths. It is a challenge to take a truthful look at ourselves

When we finally do, we often don't think about it too long or too hard. Well known in social psychology, the confirmation bias plays just as powerful a role in looking at ourselves as it does in judging others. We usually find "what we are looking for" when we do. Remarkable research studies show that people *think* they are better than they actually are in numerous areas. People tend to give themselves better ratings on their physical appearance, their driving skills (if they stop at a stop sign!) the quality impact of their teaching methods, and the success rate of their stock picks.[2,3,4]

A simple, but straight-shooting fact here is that **self examination does not equate to self-awareness**. A culture dominated by a lack of self-awareness and a tendency to inaccurately evaluate ourselves promotes collective self-involvement.

Let's take me, for an example. Therapy, coaching, education, spiritual workshops, and professional development have contributed to my self understanding. I am the type of person who likes to be social, active, curious, and engaged. I have an enthusiastic and optimistic personality. I like to solve problems "on my feet," and to exchange thoughts and ideas.

These tendencies have served me well in many situations. To describe them as strengths, however, fails to capture the entire truth. Upon closer examination, it is also true that these patterns overwhelm, distract or annoy others. Sometimes, I am unaware when they are diverting some people from what is important to them. In those contexts, they are counter-productive to connecting with others, and also can deplete my energy.

Want to know how I became aware of this? You guessed it—during a *Check In*. I had been hired to help a team quickly achieve compliance on an organizational-wide task. Leaders were stepping on each other's toes left and right. I started a meeting with this *Check In*: (See Question #32) "What do other people sometimes do that easily distracts you?" Much to my surprise, during the *Check In*, one person courageously called me out by name in his response: "When Krystal takes us in a completely different direction without informing us beforehand."

Wow. Here I am, writing this out years later, and his answer *still* motivates me to slow down the pace of change, to move with singular precision, and to fight the urge to "over-produce" at any point of time, especially in a single session. The self-awareness gained *then* helps me to manage myself *now*. It also helps me be socially aware and a better leader in similar contexts in the future. Experiencing this "aha moment" on a routine basis is how *Check In* raises our Emotional Intelligence.

Although self-awareness is necessary to be socially effective, it is insufficient. The type of EI that transforms family or team dynamics, changes organizational cultures and develops communities of mindful citizens, requires behavior change.

 *What is something that usually works for you, but isn't helping you right now?*

I led a *Check In* using the question above while writing this book. My own my answer was enlightening. My normal social engagement patterns had been distracting me from getting high-quality writing time in. Following my insight, I disciplined myself not to text, call or make appointments for the first two hours every morning until the first draft of this book was completed. I felt compelled to do something non-standard for myself: I decided to dis-engage.

Answering the question with others increased my energy to be more responsible for my own wellbeing. *Check In* requires repetition, social engagement, and follow through to optimally improve each of the four domains of EI. Following the guidelines of this book will help you do just that.

Can I Have Your Attention, Please?

Check In is a discipline that sharpens collective attention and widens shared observation. Group reflection requires "slowing down" to a certain extent. Think of it like a neighborhood speed bump—it prevents mindless accidents and amplifies our attention to the social context around us.

Our contemporary adult lives are jam packed with information, decisions, distractions and desires. Consider, if the average adult uses more than 1000 words[5], how many does she hear or read? If we make over 200 decisions involving food alone each day[6], consider the sheer amount of choices we make about our appearance, our finances, our entertainment options, our hobbies, our care-giving, our transportation. Supporting such productivity is a highly active mind. The brain takes up 90% of our energy consumption. We are almost always scanning, sensing, filtering, reacting or responding. And, we are trying to "balance it all" in the process. If you're a leader, manager, teacher, health care worker, parent, consultant or...well, an adult, you're also trying to balance this process in others!

Turns out, we just don't excel when we're trying to attend to everything. Our brain is very prone to wrong assumptions, inaccurate conclusions, and faulty beliefs, especially when we are going too fast.[7]

For adults who get paid primarily to use their "brain" power and their people skills, attention and observational capacity is either a competitive advantage or an Achilles heel[8]. Marketing research, neuroscience and wisdom teachings have told us in many different ways that: **Where our attention goes, is where our power flows.**

The Nobel prize winning economist and cognitive psychologist Herbert Simon once said:"A wealth of information creates a poverty of attention."

 *What needs your attention right now?*

Strangely, as a society we don't seem "to mind" being so impoverished. Deprivation of high quality attention certainly doesn't prevent us from heaping more helpings of stimulation and information overload onto our already full plate. We are information hoarders. The more the better, right?

Our relationships are no different. Of course modern relationships are commonly described as "complicated. There are two or more brains bombarded with "head stuff!"

We like to put our stuff in other people's brains, too. You know what I'm talking about. Think back on the last time you walked into a meeting, a dinner date, or your front door. You've got a call to make, a plane to book and/or a grocery list in your mind (or literally hanging from your forearms, which lack rock-climber robustness). The next thing you know, you encounter another person, mindlessly putting *more* stuff in your head: There's a problem with the computer, or someone else is acting like a jerk, or he has an idea for a birthday party, or wants your input about dinner (no! not another food thought!).

No wonder why relationships sometimes add to our confusion, diffusion, destabilization. At some point, the load gets so heavy, that we dump stuff, freeze or break down completely. Most of the time, we offload our information in a careless or sloppy way. We send an unthoughtful email. We complete a task hastily. We break down communication, saying things that make no sense, or is harmful to others. Sometimes, we don't say anything at all. Other times, we numb ourselves with technologies or activities that float our focus away.

Our collective information overload damages the quality of our relationships. As this cycle repeats over and over, our capacity to socially attend gets smaller and smaller. Therefore, our ability to resolve complex problems is reduced.

Our lifestyle trains us to be less relationally attentive, as well as less socially responsible. And part of our brain *really* likes that.

Before you move on. Just let that sink in for a moment. We *prefer* to be less aware much of the time to those around us. This profound truth can sting a bit if you sit with it.

Now, I know you want to move on. You probably are ready to hear what the solution is. But just stay with me for a bit longer here. We frequently, or *almost always,* do not come to a complete stop at a stop sign[9]. Most of us will not want to stay still with the pretty clear evidence that we are woefully inadequate at paying attention to some essential things, especially when it comes to social relationships. We may be competent at doing so with one other person, in a highly specific context, but add another into the mix, and then another, and then change the environment—very quickly, we reach the limits of our capacity to effectively observe, and respond to, group dynamics .

Have I lost you already?? Are you jumping to the next page? Looking for the next break? Checking your phone? Jotting down a note (mental or physical) to help you remember something?

Chances are, at some point in reading this chapter, you'll skip or glance over something. That's perfectly normal. Individual readers often vary significantly in their retention of material they learn by reading. That's where the group has *the potential* to enhance true learning. Educational psychology and learning science has demonstrated that students who study together outside the class perform better than those who study alone[10] This isn't always true when trying to learn the material in the class, however (again, we can sometimes distract others!).

Reading this book, you will miss something important that someone else will catch (especially if someone distracts you!). When we bring the best of our selective attention together, we learn better. Teams that train effectively together, perform better. It doesn't take a sports psychologist or for us to be a coach to understand that effective group training, both physical and mental, translates into higher levels of execution, and enjoyment, when the real deal (e.g. game, performance, activity) is being experienced.

Check in is a simple way to build up our attentional capacity while improving the effectiveness of our language about what we are observing. Think of it like a work-out buddy. Those who *Check In* together, improve together, but only if you do it well.

What Is It?

When authority figures say, "I need you to pay attention," what they really want is for you to use that attention in a useful way. They really should say "I need you to *observe* something."

I'll spare you from going into copious detail regarding the role neuropsychology plays here. For our purposes, you only need to know that observation is a key pillar of mindfulness[11]. Those who have a higher capacity to focus attention on what is **most** important to the group's values and goals will have an advantage in that setting. Those who attend **and also** observe, however, will not only perform better, the quality of their experiences will be better as well. They will do better **and** feel better. Hopefully, they will use this performance to lead others to improve in these areas as well.

 *Improve your selective attention to become smarter. Improve your social observation to become wiser.*

Observation is a super power available to any person willing to train for it.

You get this at a deep level. Observation often drives how fulfilled or content you feel. Are you observing something pleasing, or something upsetting? Unlike attention, which is all about the object, observation entails a significant degree of choice, of creativity, and of mindfulness.

The reality of our lives is not just what happens to us, those black or white facts: You have a meeting. You give a report. You eat lunch. You have a conversation. What we observe to happen to us, is those facts, colored in by our thoughts, feelings, needs, ideals, expectations and goals.

We often operate in reality using good-enough assumptions, interpretations, and contextual triggers. The very minds that evolved to keep us alive often lead us to be lost in the static of our minds. We habitually observe the "static" or a snapshot of what's going on, rather than take in a fuller perspective[7]. Widening our observation to "notice more" of what surrounds us, as well as what's happening in our bodies and minds, is a well-studied and frequently practiced pathway to personal development[11].

Check In is intended to provoke social observation. When done repeatedly, this observation (especially when combined with EI) is highly likely to lead to a reduction of misassumptions and failed communications, social isolation, and social stress.

Imagine you and your team are at an art exhibition at the Louvre. The experience is exciting, complex and stimulating. It's hard to prioritize. It is easy it is to get lost. Good thing you guys decided to take a guided tour. You were wise enough to do a private one so you can tailor it to the specific goals your team has right now. The guide takes you to the pieces of art that are most relevant for your team to look at. Forget the shiny objects, or even the staples that everyone else is gawking at. Your team needs to only see three to five salient pieces to get the most out of the time together. The guide selects what your team pays attention to with utmost expertise and deliberation. That's the selective attention part of the equation.

When you all are together in front of each piece of art, the guide points out what he observes. All of the sudden, your team observes it too! The guide engaged the whole group to start observing more and more. Then, one of the members shares something that is completely innovative that not even the guide had observed before. The entire art transforms in front of everyone's mind. That is collaborative innovation, the social observation part of the equation.

Very few teams have a systemic process to train for both attention and observation at the same time. Teams that are disciplined in practicing both often are the ones who *enjoy* performing well together. *Check In* is a one tool to help your team do just that.

We Pledge Allegiance

We rely on the capital of emotional connection in order to sustain any collective effort. We can be attentive and observant to social dynamics without investing our personal energy into them. Uncommitted detachment rarely sustains social effectiveness.

Engagement influences the outcome of any relational effort. It is the fuel for change--whether that change is emotional, cognitive or behavioral. At its basic level, engaged individuals emotionally commit *to do something with others.* The word "engage" comes from the French word, *engager.* The word originally meant 'to pawn or pledge something.' Then later 'pledge oneself (to do something').

It is a highly prized personal and group experience that is often talked about, yet rarely *consistently* embodied.

When is the last time you pledged to do something? What impact does that pledge have on you today?

If you find yourself a little dismayed by how recent your answer was, you're in good company. We tend to explicitly "pledge" ourselves only in highly specific circumstances: 1) In school, saying *The Pledge of Allegiance* 2) when people enter or are promoted in government, military, protective, or service-oriented professions or positions 3) in some religious or spiritual communities 4) (legal/social) contracts. There probably are a few other situations where your pledge was given. Some your pledges may have been implicit or inferred.

From the age of late adolescence onward, you have been internally driven to conscientiously pledge yourself to something worthwhile. The older we get, however, the more experiences we have where our pledges don't "pay off." We are quick to question if our engagement is worth it and we are hesitant or resistant to extend our allegiance to others.

We often underestimate how foundational this allegiance is to increase our *shared capacity* to sustain engagement, especially when challenges inevitably occur. One of the most psychologically and socially intense disciplines I train teams on is conscious "contracting." It is a form of developing a team "pledge." Most teams require **significantly** more support through this process than they expect. We aren't used to, and often don't feel safe to collectively clarify our goals and our commitments to one another.

Collective engagement is required to sustain individual engagement. Teams can have a super star performer, and/or a handful of talented staff. Individual engagement can last only for so long. Some MVPs are more committed to their own performance or goals than those of the team. Engagement of their peer's needs or interests waxes and wanes depending on what they are attending to and observing.

Many times, variation in engagement is not due to people being self-absorbed. It is because they haven't explicitly communicated and listened to one another's expectations and/or key goals.

Check In creates the necessary emotional conditions for engagement. It creates a playing field where individuals pledge to share and they pledge to receive what others share. Participants aren't usually unaware that this dynamic is occurring during the process. They don't have to be, in this context. Simply, the more others are emotionally engaged, the better it feels for those around them.

Very few people sustain high-impact, authentic interactions with us when we are more committed to our self than others. I don't consider myself as being self-focused, but I'm often lost in my own mind. When I'm overcommitted, am sleep deprived, or have low blood sugar, I am unconsciously more committed to me than anything else. Too many times I have shown up to a social interaction "unpledged" to others. I am in this state sometimes more than I care to admit (remember our tendency is to enhance our qualities). When others consciously bridge across my self-involvement, my engagement improves. This combination of observation and conscious joining is rare, however, without a system like *Check In* to guide it.

One of the impediments to achieving our allegiance is phantom engagement in others. This looks like:

- ✓ People who are talking, without really joining a shared conversation.
- ✓ People who aren't talking, but also not really listening to what's being said.
- ✓ People who we assume are committed to the same things but aren't.
- ✓ People who are committed to the same things, but are temporarily MIA due to other constraints, issues or needs.

The more we experience this pattern, the easier it is for our own behavior to follow suit. Observe any social gathering and you'll notice how easy it is to follow others. Yawning, laughing, hiccupping, talk using stereotypes. Disengagement is also contagious. For example, in education settings, when one student leaves the classroom, another student is likely to demonstrate some form is disengaging behavior[12]. When one person quits a new exercise routine, diet, or starts smoking again, those around them are statistically more likely to "quit" as well[13]. In teams who must collaborate on a project together, the group's performance is strongly related to contribution of the lowest performer[14]. Gruenter and Whitaker, leaders from the Studer Group, warn: "The culture of any organization is shaped by the worst behavior the leader is willing to tolerate"[15].

We grimly understand that the same implications hold for our personal relationships and communities. Tolerating disengagement is a bad habit that impedes connectivity across all relationships.

Disengagement at work is estimated to cost $600 billion per year in lost productivity in the US alone[16]. Although engagement is contagious, it requires much more social muscle than its opposite. Research demonstrates that positive influence takes more exposure, repetition, and recognition than negative influence.

Many of the leading CEOs, innovative and profitable start-ups and contemporary business consultants who have invested in creating a culture of engagement. This type of culture is frequently obtained by systematically raising EI throughout an organization's leadership and core teams. Given our information overload, our full schedules, and the complexities of our relationships, a sustainable process is critical to get others to keep pledging their energy to a shared goal.

Check In is a simple engagement tool that doesn't require a program, support by strategic plan, or pre-requisite communication skills.

Group Cohesion

Check In successfully checks our minds *out* of tasks, situations or plans that aren't necessary or helpful for present moment. It has a similar effect as closing open tabs on a browser or closing a door or window. It concentrates energy, making it more available for the social situation at hand.

Physically and psychologically, we can't be checked into two places at the same. Trying to be bilocated, or in two places at the same time, creates a significant demand on the brain. Few people can successfully sustain this process for a long time. We know all about the significant perils of multitasking. Despite our informed knowledge, our lifestyles habitually are geared for doing too many things at a time, in a day, without focused presence. Research has shown that bilocation, worsens individual performance[17].

When it is executed competently, *Check In* generates a form of bilocation that is advantageous to groups. With consistent exposure, individuals improve their capacity to understand others' perspectives, genuinely understand their own, *and* plan an appropriate action in response[18]. They effectively bilocate, improving group cohesion.

Interesting research in virtual platforms involving avatars indicates that some expressions of bilocation, actually boosts effective social interaction[19].

When was the last time you  *actively cooperated with your friends, coworkers or community in order to benefit everyone? Where did your energy come from?*

Group cohesion occurs when most members of a group consciously unite resources so that the group itself prospers, not any particular individual. Genuine group cohesion is correlated with improved health and financial prosperity within individuals who belong to the group.

Unfortunately, it doesn't happen without competent cultivation. If you have been part of a lot of groups or teams in the past decade, you'll agree that many groups publicize that they are cohesive when they are far from it. Relationships are prone to fake synchronization even when competition, cliques or silos, and individual interests are the norm.

A few years ago, a leader I deeply respected asked me to lead *Check In* during a run-of-the-mill monthly committee meeting. I had never attended this meeting. We determined that my role was to raise his group's engagement level and get them to "gel better." The *Check In* question I lead with was, "What could this committee do together right now that would energize you?"

The first person to answer the question provided a lackluster response. I can't remember it. An unenergized response is often a response we forget. It doesn't move us. Without energy, relationships can't bond together.

What *I do* remember are the exact words from the person who answered the question next. A typically mild mannered and quiet colleague shared something that had heat, was heartfelt and he had been thinking about for some time. It was urgent and clear. It was so compelling that at least four others repeated his theme and validated his idea. One line from his response, word for word was: "We can show them that we are listening." By the end of *Check In,* the committee was more willingness to benefit their mission. For the rest of the meeting, in a mere forty-five minutes, they developed a new process that was more cohesive for them *and* their client. At the time of writing this book, their strategy was still being used.

Starved For (Real) Recognition

As more and more people became overstimulated, overscheduled and overstressed in the last thirty years, society has moved away from promoting community activities. We invest more today in personal learning, personal style and *personal recognition.*

People like getting recognized; it tends to make them more satisfied in their relationships across all contexts—professionally, personally, romantically, even as parents (even if it only happens a few times per calendar year) "Praise in public, punish in private" as long been advised across many contexts (e.g. education, parenting, management). Receiving praise professionally often predicts staff retention and loyalty[20]. Managers tend to handle professional challenges better when they are personally recognized[21]. This performance boost is also noticeable then when staff is learning something new or in the process of an important organizational change[22,23].

Recognition comes in four main forms[24]:

✓ Personal recognition
✓ Recognition of results
✓ Recognition of work process or practice
✓ Recognition of job dedication.

In the last decade, we have seen the use of *public personal recognition,* sky-rocket in organizations, business, teams, communities and even personal relationships via social media.

This social trend has a significant dark side, however. Recognition is *so* utilized, that if a person' doesn't get recognized in some way over a certain amount of time, it discourages, confuses or irritates or sense of self-worth. Studies reveal that low or poor recognition is the second-largest risk factor for psychological distress in the workplace[25].

Organizationally speaking, we know that most organizations practice hierarchical recognition—someone "higher up" recognizes someone "lower down." This often is associated with a workforce that passively waits for recognition, or jockeys for attention at an individual or group level. It can contribute to a mindset of "we-must-please-the-people" from those at the executive level, and therefore recognize people habitually rather than deliberately or fairly.

In some work cultures, many are skeptical of the recognition our peers receive and unlikely to formally recognize one another. Peers brush off positive feedback from one another when they do get it, discounting it as mattering less compared to the value it would have if given from those have more positional authority. Finally, individuals who do win recognition often do not achieve their success without the support of many others around them. Does the person really deserve the applause?

We know what it feels like when someone is recognizing us only to get something out of us. We know when someone is recognizing someone else only because they feel obliged to. Those ways of recognizing only breaks bonds, it doesn't unite them.

Family and romantic relationships, and even friendships, are no different. This may sound like some families, platforms or communities that you've recently experienced. Ironically, all our efforts to recognize people more has left many of us genuinely recognition hungry.

Check In compensates for this current social dilemma by fostering immediate and salient recognition between peers at a genuine level. The recognition doesn't look the way most we expect it would. People don't usually express: "I like how Bob answered the question." Instead, they validate how a person made them feel, think or want to do something differently. They may repeat the theme someone else introduced, or during the debrief, they come back a group member's share.

To be direct—recognition is *not* a human need. It is a currency of our contemporary culture. People do **need a sense of belonging**. They need to believe that they can personally make a valuable contribution to the world that honors themselves and serves a group. Recognition can be used to indicate that our needs are getting met, but it's only a sign. Recognition is not a pathway and it's not a destination to meeting real human needs.

Many of us do what we do in our personal and professional settings without getting a lot of social credit for it. In fact, many people report that when they do get genuine recognition, earn an award, or receive an authentic compliment, they feel uncomfortable. We need cohesion, not necessarily recognition.

For the record, when leading a *Check In* that asks what energizes or brings joy to a person, I have never heard "When I got this award" or "When I got a promotion." I have probably done a million *Check Ins* (one time I counted more than a dozen in ONE day!). I would guess that I use this question, or a variant (See Question #11) about 15% of the time. I don't recall anyone ever mentioning personal recognition. People have reported being proud about these recognitions (See Question #16) but they usually connect recognition with energy and joy. What people do frequently name are:

✓ Relationships. Something that others do for them, or they experience with others. Examples include: When someone close to them achieved or overcome something meaningful, shared activities, being vulnerable and supported, gaining insight or mastery as a by product of social connection.

✓ Progress. Examples include: When they are making headway on a project, experiencing something new, figuring something out that is tough or complicated, or pushing hard and seeing that they are excelling past the previous mark.

✓ Health/Wellbeing. Examples included: When they engaged in an activity that nourishes or engages their physical vitality, spiritual or religious experiences, emotional or social experiences that enhance positivity or peace, when they or someone they care about recovers from an illness or positively develops

Check In recognizes a person's genuine needs, values and truth. This is helpful in a culture where achievements, genuine or not, get more press. With competent use of the tool, users are more able and willing to recognize one another's diversity, personal resilience, and vulnerability.

The Real Deal

When was the last time you faked it?

We all have faked something. We all have certain relationships, or certain situations, or certain emotional states and perspectives that trigger us to fake it. Consider some of yours.

Too often, we aren't even aware of when we are faking it. As a culture, we become so used to how things look superficially, or how we compare to others, that we forget who we are, what we stand for, and what we think is really going on. We conform mindlessly, and especially when there is social pressure[26].

Other times, we do know we are faking it. There are seasons of our lives when our brains and hormones set us up for deception, especially during our adolescent years. Eventually, our biology isn't driving the behavior anymore, and our social psychology is (although the two are *always connected*). We fake it when the situation is new, or uncertain. We fake it when we feel like a certain role demands it. We fake it to prevent disappointment to meet (perceived) expectations. We fake it to go with the flow of social convention or established norms.

When facilitated well, *Check In* invites individuals in the group to slow down and get real. Individuals are encouraged, reminded, and prompted to reflect on, and publicly share, their real answers to essential questions. This process can generate authenticity.

We crave authenticity internally. We know when we externally express it, it is helpful. People who are more authentic tend to be happier, have higher self-esteem, have more positive emotions, better relationships, more personal growth[27].

Authenticity involves
✓ Knowing who you really are.
✓ Living according to who you really are.

✓ Standing up for who you really are in spite of internal triggers and/or external influence.

We just don't know how to easily do it in our social groups, and we aren't that deliberate in our effort to achieve it.

Check In is an easy to share discipline that helps us express our authenticity at a social level. When we slow down long enough to consciously choose our responses to the questions, and are asked to share them, authenticity becomes more available

The process gives us the opportunity to:

✓ Identify our own answer
✓ Verbalize our answer socially.
✓ Question if our answer is *really* authentic as we experience the answers of others.

Often, we realize how we are deceiving ourselves when we hear others speaking their truths.

"The essence of bravery is being without self-deception."

—Pema Chödrön

Many of us flinch when experiencing a reality that is less than ideal, especially versions of ourselves that fall short of our goals or intentions or are sub-optimal than we are capable of. Reflecting on our own is often overwhelming and/or ineffective. It can provoke self-criticism, judgement, blame, guilt and shame. At first, our authentic answers can be more painful than productive. They also can temporarily inhibit performance.

It's easy to beat up on yourself. But it's also easy to let yourself off the hook. Our relationships can prevent these extremes if we train them to. Because we are so used to projecting a certain version of ourselves, rather than being ourselves, we need routines that invite us to be real with one another and be also compassionate.

When we get real with ourselves and choose to share with others who are willing to listen, trust increases. Listening to others who are open and real is clearly helpful; and the majority of people enjoy helping others in need. Research shows that the same area of our brain is active when we are truly helping others as when we are gratifying a personal desire[28].

The wise encouragement that: "If you don't have anything nice to say, don't say anything at all" has been twisted from its original intent to foster social skills. Verbalizing your truth carefully is perhaps the nicest thing you can do for yourself, and your relationships. Especially those relationships where you have agreed do something important together.

Relationships that converse openly and compassionately tend to be the ones that are more likely to master conflict and sustain commitment during challenging circumstances[29].

While I was writing this book, I was having dinner one night with two friends. One I have known a few months and the other I had known many years. The new friend had never done a *Check In* before, and the other had done more than twenty-five with me.

Share something that you want more of in this season of your life. What difference does that make?

This was our question. The friend familiar with *Check In* volunteered to start. I won't share our answers, as they were quite personal and very authentic. What I will share is how easy, fun, real and refreshing the rest of our time together was. After *Check In*, we discussed how we all desire more experiences in social groups where we share and listen at the meaningful level we just did.

My new friend asked my old one what Check In was like when he first encountered it. He shared that he never achieved absolute comfort with the process, but he felt others did. He felt that the value of trust it brought to the group was worth his personal discomfort. He also described that he tends to answer the questions openly and concretely, compared to some others who answer more conceptually or with emotion. He told her that people who usually answered one way, would sometimes surprise his expectations and answer in a completely different style.

Check In, if we are really keeping it real, will be as dynamic and diverse as people are. Not just between individuals, but within them.

My dinner guests and I agreed that in many other situations, the reality of our social interactions does not match up our experience that evening at dinner. Not every *Check In* will either. But when it does, you will feel it and you will want more of it. Some days, *Check In* may be the only part of the day when individuals feel understood and accepted. That should be enough motivation for us to use the tool consistently in the relationships essential to us and our work together.

CHAPTER THREE

How To *Check in*

Start how you want to finish.
If you get anything from this book, take away this one thing—discerning your intention, and attending to it, are the two most essential components of improvement. We must clarify what we desire, give it our attention, and then actively try out new behaviors designed to fulfill them.

The word "desire" itself comes the Latin form of the word desiderate, which literally means to be away from a star. Science acknowledges that all life requires this type of energy. Yet many of us find it challenging to go after what we truly desire without feeling selfish, demanding, or unrealistic. Many people are hesitant to not only follow their desires, but to acknowledge they have them in the first place.

Achieving the best result with *Check In* relies on you to clarify what outcome you desire. Not what you want to say, or the question you want to ask, but the impact you want to have by using it to begin with.

 *By the end of our time together, what would you like to have experienced, changed or learned?*

When *Check In* is completed, and you move on to whatever comes next, something should be different as a result. Every *Check In* is a deposit, a vote, or an investment towards the kind of future you want your relationships to have.

If you are unsure of what your intention is for *Check In* (or your day, your vacation, your dinner date) don't worry. You're normal. If you or feel uncertain about how to identify your intentions, rest assured that this also is quite normal. Clarifying your true desires and deciphering your real needs is not something that comes natural to any individual. Not is it a skill many people are trained in. Transferring self-awareness into practical skills *doesn't happen without practice*. We need methods to turn newly acquired ideas into actual behaviors you can easily repeat. Many times, our habits don't convey anything about our desires, however.

Why do something if you don't know what you really want from it? You have motivations that are undiscovered, desires that are undeciphered, and inspirations that are unborn. So does everyone around you. *Check In* offers a practical way to recognize them.

Spending time practicing desired outcome identification and effective intentionality is highly recommended while you also are learning to lead *Check In.* An easy way to do this is spending five minutes before your day asking yourself a variant of the question asked on page 64.

In terms of using this tool, figure out what the group needs before you select a question. Start with identifying this intention, then choose between the many questions at the back of the book. This outcome could be a feeling, a goal, a product, a state or an idea.

Before I fill your head with some structured outcomes from my own expertise, I want you to use your own very capable and wise imagination.

✓ What does this group need more of?
✓ What does it need less of?
✓ How do I want the group to feel, think or act right now?
✓ What role do I want to play in this process right now?
✓ What *Check In* question ill compel us closer or further from these things?

Some people name what they want to stop first, and then back track to consider what exactly they want more of. Other people work the opposite way. Notice what way is easiest for you and try practicing the other way.

Return to these reflections frequently to gain clarity.

Now that you've taken the opportunity to reflect on your own, here are some of the outcomes people frequently desire:

- ✓ A Better understanding of who people are.
- ✓ More positivity, humor or camaraderie.
- ✓ More motivation and energy for work.
- ✓ More diversity in how people feel, think and act.
- ✓ More prosocial, or collaborative behaviors.
- ✓ More creativity, innovation, competence.
- ✓ More group commitment and buy in.
- ✓ More solutions to complex problems.
- ✓ More personal awareness.
- ✓ More personal responsibility or ownership.
- ✓ Less conflict between specific individuals.
- ✓ Less division between teams/departments.
- ✓ Less group think and cognitive biases.
- ✓ Less personal isolation or withholding information.
- ✓ Less selfish and toxic thoughts, feelings, actions.
- ✓ Less disengagement, mediocre performance.

The first main "rule" of *Check In* is to discern what you want, why you want it, and then choose the question. Keep your intention in your attention throughout the entire process. Your intention is vehicle and your attention is the fuel. You need both to get your group to where they need to go. Choose and use both consciously.

Just Do It

Facilitating *Check In* is a skill. The more you practice the skill, the more competent, and confident you will become. After setting and following your intention, the most important part of how to *Check In* involves leading checking in routinely. If you don't do it consistently, you won't get better. If you are inconsistent, others won't benefit. Like many other skills, they try it a few times, and even though it feels good and there is clear benefit, they forget to do it again. If it isn't used, or isn't modeled, it doesn't ingrain itself into the routine of everyday practice. This book can help people learn the skill, but it is limited in its ability to transition the skill into competent, consistent use. To do so, it requires the power of proactive learner and social observation. Training and coaching from those who have mastered the skill is always a catalyst for improvement (See Resources.)

Clarified Intention
+
Consistent Practice
+
Social Observation
=
Improved Performance.

One thing I value about this tool is that consistency is not equated to rigidity. Because our intentions are diverse, our questions must change. Because our people are diverse, our must results change. The tool in and of itself provides consistent stability for the team without defaulting to dogma.

The good news is that if you consistently follow the guidelines in this chapter during your learning of the tool, you *will* quickly master it. It may take more discipline for some to use the guidelines with a group. Some people fear that they may look overbearing or too structured, or they may do it "wrong." Sharing the guidelines with the group may take less effort for those who prefer or are used to providing structure and clear guidance. Some of them may need more practice on how to use the guidelines without being over controlling or inapproachable.

Visit www.joincheckin.com to download a printable copy of the guidelines for free. There are two sizes available: one for you to use as a self-reference, and one for the group to use as a visual reference. Take into consideration your capacity as a public speaker, the context of the group and your desired outcome for using the printed guidelines. This document can serve as a visual reminder of the guidelines, but only you can discern the other key components of the tool.

Giving The Check In Question

Your method for how to share the question you select will vary. Are most people in the group familiar with the guidelines? Where are you and what time of day is it? How large is the group? You will learn more about these variables in the following chapters.

Here are ideas to present the question:

✓ Say the question out loud. This works well in groups of 4 people or less, which includes you as the facilitator.

✓ For larger groups, share the question orally *and* in writing. You can:
- Visually reference the question page in the back of this book
- Give it in the body of the calendar invite
- Present it at the top of the printed agenda
- Write is on a single presentation slide
- Write it out on a white board
- Write it on multiple index cards

✓ Share the question only in writing. This is best done if each person has it printed out and if the group is familiar with the process.

Get The Party Started!

Your group should be ready to begin by this point. Ask for a volunteer to start. There usually is one person in a group that (sometimes unconsciously) always wants to go first. Likewise, there is another who rarely wants to start. A facilitator doesn't need to control this natural group dynamic when first learning *Check In*. More advanced *Check In* facilitators may want to bring it to the group's attention in the debrief. We will address how to debrief below, and some issues may be answered in the problem shooting section.

For now, focus on how you ask for one person to begin. Some suggestions are:

✓ "Someone please start *Check In*
✓ "Some please answer first"
✓ "Who wants to begin/go first?"
✓ "Who will volunteer?"

Be The leader

Leadership often requires reminding people of guidelines and shared standards. It's important to remember that most people are inattentive, distracted or over stimulated in group situations. People don't need you to remind them of the guidelines because they are resistant or don't care. We need our leaders to focus our attention and inspire group engagement.

If you do enough *Check Ins*, there will always come a time when someone interrupts another person or makes a comment despite being directed to only listen. When this happens, a good facilitator will pause a bit to notice how the rest of the group responds to this occurrence. Sometimes, another person in the group, or the offender herself, will quickly redirect. Sometimes, those who don't like the guidelines being disregarded will nonverbally the send message to "be quiet." Often, if the group is larger than seven or so people, at least one person will visually look back at the facilitator, or another key authority figure in the group, to see if he or she "will do anything about it."

This is an opportunity to build or break the group trust. Will you step in and ensure that group upholds the standards that *you've said* are important to achieve the group's results? If you're like many of us, you will find yourself challenged

I typically not verbally respond to a non distracting comment when it first occurs. I always will make eye contact with the person, however. After a few times, I'll step in and remind people of the guidelines. The tone of how I step in depends on the group dynamic, namely—how much trust the group has built with me and with one another. Sometimes I'll point to the guideline without saying anything. Holding up my hand or shaking my head "No" often works. What I say doesn't matter, as long as it is concise. Examples:

- ✓ "Just listen"
- ✓ "Stay within yourself"
- ✓ "Hold on"
- ✓ "Wait for it"

Make It Matter

What the group takes away, or actively remembers from *Check In* often is determined by the quality of the debrief. The purpose of the debrief is to increase the awareness of and attention to your selected intention. When or where did they notice more or less presence, engagement, compassion, cohesion, energy, authenticity?

After everyone has answered the question, including the facilitator, the group attends to any important comments, shared experiences or questions. Some suggestions for starting the debrief:

- ✓ "Does anyone want to share what his/her experience was like during *Check In?*"
- ✓ "Is there something important you heard that we should come back to as a whole group?"

The engagement of the group in enriching discourse after *Check In* relies heavily effective facilitation, the group size, how many times others have used the tool, and whether individuals verbalize when they are curious or share their authentic thoughts/feelings. Most groups over six people will often have at least one individual who answers a version of the prompts above. He or she will typically ask another person a question or relate to something another person shared. Other times, an individual will come back to clarify or change something she herself offered. Sometimes, this is an indicator of that *Check In* stimulated deeper understanding, or social influence. A facilitator should ask that person what motivate the person to share differently, or more, now. What was it about the group experience that gave them a different perspective? This brings attention that *Check In* fosters synergy and awareness that the group influences the individual and the individual influences the group.

Sometimes, an individual will ask the facilitator questions or take the group in an entirely different direction. It is easy for the facilitator to get in a Q and A session with this person, or to move ahead to the agenda of the day. Debrief is meant to amplify a specific group result. Ask the group "what do you guys think?" before inserting your answer. If the group wants to speed ahead, slow them back down: "Before we jump ahead, let's finish *Check In*." Make sure to make any points you have about the group dynamics and your desired intention before moving on.

Out of all the steps in *Check In*, the debrief requires the most practice to master. Focus on the steps of using the tool before delving too deeply in this step. Make a point about something you saw that is worthy of recognition, or something that you did not see that is, that is directly connected to the result you intend. Then, move on.

The Buddy System

If you are devoted to mastering the tool as quickly as possible, ask a trusted person to support your improvement at leading *Check In*. This person would pay attention to how effective you are a guiding the group to achieve the result you want. This extra step requires that 1) you identify your intention and 2) express it effectively to the person supporting you and 3) that person is capable and willing to support you and participate in *Check In* at the same time.

Most of the leaders who try to learn *Check In* do not routinely ask for feedback on how effective they are at leading it. The ones that do, however, quickly advance in their capacity to use the tool for its maximum social benefits.

Follow the guidelines and the best practices for each step of *Check In*, and you **will observe** positive results. Keep trying it out, noticing what works and doesn't work for yourself and your group. Paying attention to the context and the timing will be extremely helpful in catalyzing your learning. The next chapters explore these areas.

Step 1. Determine your intention.

Step 2. Select a question that *best* supports this intention.

Step 3. Inform the group of how the tool works. How you introduce, explain and facilitate check in should be unique to your style, brand and mood. Make sure that you include the guidelines.

Step 4. Share the *Check In* question.

Step 5. Ask for a volunteer to go first.

Step 6. Step in when there is someone who doesn't follow the guidelines.

Step 7. Debrief the group with your intention in mind.

Extra credit: Ask one person in the group to give you feedback after the entire meeting is over.

Check In Sample Scripts
Professional Settings

"We're going to start our time with a process called *Check In*. (I just read an amazing book, you should go out there and read it too! People will love you. It will save your teams!). Check in helps teams be more present, engaged and synchronized. It is a structured way we can express ourselves and to listen to each other. Here is how it works

- ✓ The leader selects a question
- ✓ Everyone present answers the question
- ✓ There is no right way or wrong way to answer. How you interpret the question is up to you. How you answer is up to you.
- ✓ When a person is answering, please just listen. Do not interrupt, do not ask questions, do not make comments. Just receive what that person wants to share.
- ✓ After everyone has checked in, you can come back to something that was shared and discuss it as a group
- ✓ Someone volunteers to answer the question first.
- ✓ When we each finish answering the question, we call on who we'd like to hear from next
- ✓ Any questions?"

Personal Settings

Although this book focuses on *Check In* in the professional sense you can of course use the questions outside of work. Usually the opening is more casual.

"I have a conversation routine that helps people connect and communicate better. It's Called Check-In. I'd like to try it together. Here is how it works
   ✓ Someone selects a question
   ✓ Everyone here answers it, one at a time.
   ✓ One of us goes first.
   ✓ When you're finished answering, you call on who you'd like to hear from next
   ✓ There is no right way or wrong way to answer. How you interpret the question is up to you. How you answer is up to you.
   ✓ .When a person is answering, the rest of us can only listen. Don't ask them questions or make comments. Just receive what that person wants to share.
   ✓ After everyone has checked in, we can share whatever else we want to say.
   ✓ Any questions of how it works?"

Guidelines

- ✓ The leader selects a *Check In* question.
- ✓ Each person present answers it.
- ✓ There is no right way or wrong way to answer. How you interpret the *Check In,* is up to you. How you answer it, is up to you.
- ✓ When a person is answering, just listen. Do not interrupt, do not ask questions, do not make comments. Just receive what that person wants to share.
- ✓ To start, someone volunteers to go first
- ✓ When you are finished answering, each person calls on who they want to hear from next
- ✓ After everyone has checked in, we can come back to something important that was shared or ask follow-up questions.
- ✓ Any questions about the process?

CHAPTER FOUR

Where To Do
Check In

L ocation. Location. Location. Where you are influences where you can go and how you are going to get there. Your location highly influences the readiness, the responsiveness, and the result of your *Check In*. In fact, it often is a hidden force in how the human mind and social behavior interact with one another.

We all know that where something is made often determines its value. This process driven mindset rose to more prominence in post-World War II culture. International exposure and commerce inspired us to focus on enhanced quality over sheer quantity. As branding became more and more dominant, the details of how and where things are made also became more valuable in our social mindset. It is noteworthy that during the same period, our culture also began a quest to understand and control our own minds, bodies, self-esteem, and behavior. As a location-driven lifestyle and branding rose in our commercial and social experience, we also wanted to better understand our internal, personal landscapes.

This context fascination soon extended to every area of our lives. We raced to space, rebelled against unjust social environments, explored family dynamics, and made movies about making movies. We pursued a purpose driven life, church, family, school. We created strategic plans and processes hoping they would lead to better qualitative outcomes—even if they were determined by quantitative outputs. We said, "it's not what you say it, it's how you say it." We worked to discern our "why."

Many adults also seek to discern why they do what they do and/or discover their unique existential purpose. We believe the answers touch every part of our existence. What we often don't consider is how our process of determining our answers is highly contextually dependent. We focus so much on how things work, that **we fail to discern how things are working together with the environment**. *How* you said it is *very much related* to how the person before you said it, or how hot the room was when you were saying it, or if you can see the leader's face while sharing.

Your process improvement plan will only take you so far. If you want to perform better as a human, you need a context improvement plan.

Context Is King

Our internal contexts dominate many of our social behaviors and our social relationships dominate much of our internal functioning.

Environmental contexts change how people perceive information. We perceive things to be a good deal if we see their original prices versus their discounted price. Certain lights, smells, sounds in an environment make us more likely to linger longer, buy more, and feel more safer than others. Ever walk into a restaurant and suddenly don't want to be there? We may not be aware of even the vibe we were seeking until we found ourselves in a place that doesn't work for us. Most people don't pay attention to contextual cues, but once they do, they quickly observe them everywhere.

To get good at leading *Check In,* it is key for you to pay attention to the way **context changes how people perceive one another.** Context influences people to either see people as part of their own group (the "Us" effect) or not part of their own group (the "Them" effect). People who we perceive to be more "like Us" get a lot of perceptual benefit[36]. The opposite holds true as well. Numerous research studies, some serious and some entertaining, have demonstrated this effect. One example: Give a person a cup of warm liquid and they are likely you rate you as being warm. Give a person a cup of cold liquid and they are more likely to rate you as being cold[37].

Personalities, social behavior and habits shifts widely between individuals as well as groups, all depending on the context. Hierarchy, group membership, and the cultural rules/biases of a team all contribute to its overall performance. Observe a guy at work and may see him talk for 85% of the meetings he attends, deny the request of this staff to pilot a new software program, and try to off load most tasks that he doesn't enjoy. Observe him at home, however, and you'd may see him patiently listening to his partner, planning a different vacation this year at the request of his teenagers, and doing most of the housework.

Leaders Change The Context

Great leaders not only believe that context matters, they actively optimize or change it. They don't just communicate their thoughts, feelings or directions. Before doing so, they consider the environment that their audience is in when they are receiving the message. They don't just come to a decision and then execute a strategy. They work to envision how others will perceive their actions will be perceived given the current conditions. Understanding how context works, and committing to working with it consciously, helps leaders be better servants to those who follow them.

Transformative people are the ones who change contexts. In fact, they sometimes work to change the context before they try to change a process or a person. It's similar to banning electronic use in bedrooms to help us sleep better, putting toys and magazines in waiting rooms to help us be patient, or studying abroad to appreciate diversity. Physical ones can be the most noticeable, but social contexts more potent. Leaders who notice the not so obvious cues of context, and help others around them do the same, are the ones that are going to have more prosocial influence in social settings.

Location Suggestions For *Check In*

✓ Declutter the physical space.

People act more friendly, are calmer and are more focused in physical settings that are visually open. We naturally prefer rooms with high ceilings, natural light and softer colors. Unfortunately, many of the spaces we frequently occupy, especially at work, cue people to be disengaged and closed off. Our homes can fall into this state as well. Even as I'm writing this, I am removing clutter from my desk. My own home "style" changed completely once I started devoting my professional attention to group-based leadership training. Given that I was responsible to change the context at work, I also started seeing the benefit of changing it at home.

Many of us can't go around permanently changing the décor in our professional spaces. If you don't have authority over big projects, that doesn't mean to you can't request changes from people that do. Many families and teams have experienced a significant reduction or increase in social problems following changes in physical surroundings.

As much as possible, tidy the physical space where you are doing *Check In*. Stash away objects that are distracting or appear to clutter. Remove large objects that separate people. When there are large physical objects between us, people's response to each other's nonverbal cues is slightly impeded. Doing so is likely to increase eye contact.

✓ Make it "roomy."

People are feel more at ease and open when there is the right amount of room between them and others. Too far away, and their brains are more likely to shift into seeing others as "them." Too close, and their brains start wanting to push people away. Although we each have a personal preference, the range for this preference is small. Arms length apart is the most optimal arrangement.

Notice before you start if people are clumped together or too far apart. Directly ask for people to spread out, or to move closer together. Do this if people are seated or standing. Do this a few times with the same people and it is likely that the group will start to arrange themselves with an optimal amount of room.

✓ Form a circle.

Circles convey a sense of unity. Watch a group of children playing and you'll notice that they frequently form a circle. When we are huddled, quickly access communication compared to being in a line. We tend to associate circles with positivity, openness, friendliness[38]. A circle is also helpful because it invites people to look at one another, which often cues us to perceive one another as individuals rather than objects occupying space. The "oh-they are human too" effect in the brain is more easily activated[38].

On the other hand, a circle does not force eye contact, which may trigger a biological context of flight, flight or freeze depending on what is nonverbally or verbally being communicated. Circles give people ample leeway to look away respectfully in moments of high-emotion.

In our modern society, some adults are uncomfortable sitting in a circle. In and of itself, the arrangement can trigger negative associations or memories we have with education, religious groups, therapy groups that required circle sharing. We should be mindful of the potential effect a circle has for some people. That does not mean that we should avoid forming one. Most people are likely to not mind a circle the more open their peers are and the more attentive their *Check In* leaders is. As the facilitator of *Check In*, notice what comes up for *you* asking people to get in a circle. Do you lack confidence? Think it's silly? Feel compelled to overly explain yourself? Try to deny, dismiss or avoid the resistance in others that might be present? Or do you not think about it all, and assert your authority without questioning the impact it might have on others?

Try *asking* people to form a circle once in a while and you'll probably learn a thing or two about yourself as a leader, as well as about your team. It is a simple, spontaneous exercise that can reveal some helpful information to you.

If you do *Check In* using a circle for the first time with a group, it could be a good idea to bring the "circle effect" up as a possible group observation during the debrief. Invite a comment or two about how being asked to form a circle went for them. Some of the group will inevitably say it was a little strange for them, noting it's uncommon to do at work unless you are already sitting around a table. Some may say that it reminded them of a certain place or experience. Others may shake their heads as if they were saying "I don't know what you're talking about, I crochet in circles routinely." If this occurs, use one of the major golden rules of *Check In*, just listen. You don't have to convince them that circles are awesome spiritual and psychological configurations of unity. Instead, validate that diversity is present. Making this observation public is a great contextual point to make; especially if the *Check In* result was to increase divergent thinking.

✓ No hiding.

Guide people to not hide behind other people or things. Who really enjoys sitting in the front row? Most people, even extroverts, avoid sitting in the front row. Of course, we know that if we sit up front, we can't goof off or displace our attention. But most of us even avoid sitting in the front row of movie theaters, where no one really is paying attention to our front row behavior. We also don't like being stared at from behind.

One of my personal pet peeves is when someone reads something over my shoulder. First, unless they are younger than twelve years old, they are likely to be taller than me (I stand 61.5 inches tall). The peering down at me activates an internal biological sense of being inferior, no matter how agile my mindset is at that moment. Second, it feels like they are checking up on or checking out what I am doing. No one really likes to be monitored without permission. It isn't just in our minds, it goes against our physical survival instincts.

During *Check In*, we want people *to be able* to see every one's faces. When you see someone sitting in the back row, or trying not to be seen, make it clear that people shouldn't have their backs to anyone. Keep saying either one of these statements until the desired result is achieved. Often, you'll be surprised that others shift their space to make room for every one, as much as possible, to be seen.

Where Not To Lead *Check In*

Some environments and locations should be avoided. These typically are spaces where you cannot manage interference, distraction, or voyeuristic others. These factors would most likely reduce the group's attention, attunement and appreciation of the process. Ask yourself id you could easily use another physical space for *Check In*. If not, you're advised to NOT use the tool.

Locations that may not be helpful:

- ✓ Hallways (unless it is not accessible to other parties)
- ✓ Places with so much noise participants would need to raise their voices in order to be heard
- ✓ Places with frequent over head announcements
- ✓ Spaces cluttered with physical objects
- ✓ Spaces with many visual distractions (TVs, phones, an art gallery)

These physical contexts promote the result you want *Check In* to achieves. The standard is that people are cued to see each other and be seen by one another, at least physically.

Leaders who perform the best are the ones who create awesome emotional contexts for others as well. Beyond mastering the technique (which you read about in the last chapter) you as the *Check In* leader can help do that by continually using the right questions, at the right time, with the right people. Each of these are described further in the remaining chapters.

CHAPTER FIVE

When To Do
Check In

Time waits for no one.
All adults living in Western cultures are significantly influenced by timing. The clock often reigns over our thinking, feeling and behavior. *When* something is experienced will significantly impact our biology, mind and emotions, not to mention our external performance. These dynamics are overt as well as hidden.

All of us have done the right thing in the right environment, but the timing was wrong. These experiences are emotionally disappointing and socially taxing. We take into consideration when something should be done to prevent inefficient effort and unmet expectations. *Consideration* is the operative word here. Many of us no longer merely consider time, we obsess about it, we worship it, we prove our worth through it, and we compete against it. Many of us equate freedom with being able to have full control over our calendar on a full time basis.

Many of us who have experienced having the opportunity to design our day as we deem fit will divulge—it's not as freeing as we thought it would be.

In order to use *Check In* at the right time, we need to be mindful of how we usually interact with time and it usually interacts with us. This chapter helps us do both.

Do you sometimes feel better about yourself if you accomplish something within a time goal you set? Do you sometimes feel worse about yourself if you fail to meet your own time expectations?

In our minds, effective time utilization is often used as a way to measure how responsible we are. Today, we equate time with money (or value). We used to only brag about how much money we saved, made, or how far our dollar stretched. Now, we *also* boast about how much time we saved, found, or how far our time stretched We are quick to make judgements regarding choices that we perceive are "a waste of money" or are "worth the time."

These mindsets influence how to interact with others as well.

Consider how you spend your money versus how you spend your time.

What is the impact of your expenditures?

Is time money? Is money time? There are emotional, behavioral, social and even physiological side effects to your beliefs.

Since the industrial era, adults have been shaped to manage time like we manage money. We over-spend, under-spend, tighten the reigns, mindlessly let it go. And just like our relationship with money, time often manages us. It powerfully shapes our stress levels, our sense of worth, how competent we perceive ourselves to be, where our attention (power!) goes, and drive social comparisons.

A key difference between money and time, however, is the luck factor. Many of us believe we are lucky or unlucky when it comes to timing. On the other hand, most Americans believe that if a person works hard, she can make more money. We are prone to place control outside of us when it comes to time, and within ourselves when it comes to money. Most adults take ownership of their money problems in a way that we just do not do with time.

Try out this exercise below. It will take you about 5 minutes. Think about all the ways you spent your money in the last month. Think about where it went. What percentage went to supporting your household? Your romantic interest/partner? Your family? Your friendships? Your physical upkeep? Your mental/spiritual wellbeing? Your work? Entertainment/Hobbies? Other? All of these areas need to add up to 100.

Now, for each category, estimate if the money you spent there tended to be MORE Intentional or LESS intentional. Was it deliberately chosen before you spent it with a *specific result in mind* more often or less often? Circle M for more and L for less.

Some of you formally track your money expenditures. *Use your mind* first to complete this exercise, and then reference your tracker. Discrepancies could be insightful.

House _____ % of money M/L

Love _____ % of money M/L

Family _____ % of money M/L

Friendships _____ % of money M/L

Body _____ % of money M/L

Wellbeing _____ % of money M/L

Work _____ % of money M/L

Hobbies/ _____ % of money M/L

Entertainment   **[Total = 100%]**

What thoughts came up as you completed this exercise? How much editing did it require? Why?

Now complete the same chart again, but this time reflect on your time expenditures. Spend only two minutes on this exercise. Circle M for more and L for less.

House _____ % of time   M/L

Love _____ % of time   M/L

Family _____ % of time   M/L

Friendships _____ % of time   M/L

Body _____ % of time   M/L

Wellbeing _____ % of time   M/L

Work _____ % of time   M/L

Hobbies/ _____ % of time   M/L

Entertainment

[Total = 100%]

What thoughts came up as you completed this exercise? How much editing did you do? Why?

How Time Works

Did you *really* do those exercises, or did you skip ahead?

Here is the cold, hard truth about time—when left to our own management, most people will not take the time to self-reflect, even when it is "given" to us. We skip over self-improvement exercises and reflection questions even if we believe the material is valuable to answer.

My best friend, a retired Army Nurse Officer, taught me that: **Doers Do, What Checkers Check.**

Perhaps one of the *most essential* benefits of *Check In* is that we are motivated to use the time offered to us for the purposes of reflection. Believe me, you're more likely to answer these questions when I am sitting in front of you than reading them here. The tool gives us an easy process to follow through on our desired to be conscious thinkers, feelers, doers, dreamers and leaders.

If you did do the exercises, you get bonus points! How much time did each of those exercises take? Just guess. It should have taken no more than ten minutes. Many people will ignore the instruction to take less time on the second exercise, spending the same amount or more time on it. Logically speaking, however, you should have performed faster the second time around considering the prompt, previous exposure and following an almost identical process.

Despite guidance, people usually take *longer* to complete tasks then directed or is necessary, unless there is someone physically present and reminding them how much time they have left. Think about the last time you followed a recipe that said total time required was twenty minutes and you spent close to double that amount!

People often spend more time than they expect to complete tasks or come to a decision. They often need more time than they are given or ask for as well. They often think that *other* people take less time than they do to perform similar tasks. Our experience and research clearly indicates that most people, despite their intelligence levels or technical expertise, are poor predictors of time. Even with repetitive experience of numerous tasks taking *much* longer than originally planned, we continue to falsely estimate our own time needs.[30]

We center our lives to function around use of the clock, but really are absent minded when it comes to how we interact with it.

How we concretely identify and measure time hasn't changed for centuries, but our feeling of time completely has. When we traversed on foot or horseback, the range of perceived timeliness was in months, or even entire seasons. With the invention and mass deployment of cars, aircrafts, and public transportation through our communities, our range of an acceptable time frame changed to a few weeks or days. Today, the wide-spread utilization of technology has shifted our expectation towards hours, minutes or even instant gratification.

When it comes to time, humans aren't logical; they are instinctual.

Despite our powerful instincts, we tend to forget to reference them when it comes to time. Our culture, especially our "work" or professional cultures, often dilute our natural, and often accurate, instincts. We frequently cram our desired goals to fit a certain block of time rather than the other way around. We want to get healthy so we hire a personal trainer. Session lasts an hour. We want to have a better marriage, so we go to a counselor. Session lasts an hour. We want to get on the same page and spread information, so we huddle. Another meeting or activity starts at the top of the hour, so the session lasts twenty-two minutes.

Are you also thinking "this IS way of living is kinda crazy!" Somehow, as a collective, we all have decided that what the clock or calendar says matters *more* than the results we say we want. This priority on time numbs us from actually focusing on our toughest challenges and connecting with the people around us.

Like money, time is not a mere transaction. You don't buy a Rolex to tell you the time. You buy it to express your ability to be part of historical excellence. Wearing it shapes how you think about yourself (for better or worse) and simultaneously influences how you are perceived by others. You don't *really* get what you pay for. You get what you *feel* you're paying for. Like money, the true impact of our time doesn't rely on the functionality of the object obtained. The impact relies on how the time makes people feel.

It's accurate to say: "*Check In* takes time." Whether it takes "too much time" is related to our conventional mindset about time and our standards of interacting with it. The leader of *Check In* will need to leverage these perspectives and the timing of the tool, so that the group is more willing to invest in it.

An effective *Check In* leader leverages time the way traders who make millions of dollars on the stock market leverage money. Invest in it at the right time, when the price is low, to reap the benefits down the road, when the price is high. Buyer beware: It may feel like a big risk.

How To Work Time

Most of us love blaming timing as the force of success, failure, synergy or isolation. We understand it influences our personalities, our bank accounts, our traveling efficiencies and our love lives.

Great leaders distinguish timing from luck. Timing is something we actively give. Luck is something we gratefully receive. These people don't believe they are at the mercy of time. Nor do they believe they are in an eternal competition with it. They don't micro-manage it and they don't just "flow with it." They believe that time is on their side. They actively observe its influence and they influence it back.

Timing often (ha!) is the make or break component of something performing well and something not working out. Understanding how timing works, and committing to working with it in non-standard ways, is a contribution to any improvement strategy. When you use *Check In* considering how time works, you will free yourself of the time tyranny mentality

Understand The Keys To Timing

Here is what you need to know about timing in order to optimize the impact of *Check In*:

- ✓ We instinctually prefer starts over endings. People like beginnings compared to being "in the middle" of things. Research across multiple disciplines gives much evidence for this cognitive bias.
- ✓ People trust their first impressions, or first belief or understanding about a place, a situation, person/group of people, or material. These impressions are persistent even when contradictory evidence is provided.
- ✓ People are more compliant with new diets, exercise regimes or any significant lifestyle change at the beginning.

✓ Attention is often naturally better at the start of a day, a lesson, meeting, commute, chapter/movie/album. This impacts what we recall. (my intro better be good this time!)
✓ First born children often experience multiple benefits that their siblings don't.

The preference for beginnings impacts the functioning of all social groups:

✓ Couples who recount more positive aspects about the first part of their romantic relationship are more likely to be together in a few years compared to those who recall less positive starts.
✓ Employee satisfaction during the first 30 days of being on the job is correlated with their level of engagement and productivity for the duration of their employment with an organization.
✓ Your mood in the first few hours of the day tends to persist well into the later hours, despite any "self-care" or feel good experiences mid-day.

Explore the Endnotes for specific resources[31, 32, 33, 34]. Based on this research, Check In is best used when:

✓ You have a routine morning meeting
✓ Building a new relationship with a person

- ✓ You are trying to "start again" with a pre-existing one
- ✓ You are beginning a new collaboration or pitching a new strategy
- ✓ A new person comes into a team or organization
- ✓ Leading groups of people who are coming together for the first time. (We could mistakenly call these *check-ins* Ice-breakers. I'll offer more on what those really are in a few pages.)

One other thing you need to know about time: humans instinctually, we prefer social experiences free from the pressure of it.

When time isn't a driving force or the main focus point of an interaction, we can relax and enjoy ourselves better. We also perform better cognitively, emotionally and behaviorally. Elite athletes often describe the feeling that when they are in the peak of their top performance that "the game slows down." During states of being engaged, and also unconstrained by a clock, the brain produces more feel good chemicals. Those chemicals are necessary for our health and the wellbeing of our relationships.

We naturally like this effect is because it is exclusive. Few activities and social interactions engender this "Flow State"[35]. It is highly likely that teams who experience "flow" during *Check In* will also experience a boost in positive, collaborative products outside of the time and physical space the actual *Check In* occurred.

Based on this knowledge, use *Check In more frequently* when:

✓ The team appears to lack dynamic energy or engagement
✓ Your group lacks mental diversity
✓ You need your group to be more creative, out of the box thinkers
✓ You want to foster innovation
✓ The team recently has been bombarded with tasks and deadlines

A final warning about time: people hate feeling "behind" schedule or that they are "missing out" on something happening at the same time, elsewhere.

Deep work is "Professional activity performed in a state of distraction-free concentration that push your cognitive capabilities to their limit. These efforts create new value, improve your skill, and are hard to replicate.[34]" People who earn a living primarily based on how they think adore deep work, whether it is on their own or with others.

We don't take the time for Flow or Deep Work because we feel pressured. In our minds, not obsessing about time can feel like a psychological credit card. Our cognitive biases believe that the amount of "free" time we took earlier will need to be paid later, often with a high interest charge.

Many people fear that this will cause havoc in other areas of their productive, normally scheduled, fast paced lives.

Here are the few strategies effective *Check In* leaders can do to navigate time cognitive biases

✓ Explicitly speak to people's time anxiety. Inform the group upfront "This *Check In* may take more time than we expect or even feel comfortable with. Understand that this conversation is the priority right now."

✓ Have a wide variety of Check Ins. Examine the questions and follow your instincts on which ones, if you used them right now, with this group of people, would take longer than others.

When To Use *Check In*

Traditional beginnings. *Check In* creates the best impact during routine social starts. It helps frame the group's mentality for the remainder of their experience together. When people know that they are expected to verbally contribute something from the onset of the time together, the social insight is potent. It often creates a "wake up call" to their emotional and logical centers that shifts people from a state of passivity to active participation. This is one reason why *Check In* can helps boost afternoon meeting alertness. Ever notice what happens during a meeting that starts between 1:30 and 3pm? Most people experience a hormonal and digestive lull that promotes sleepiness and diffused thinking. If the group size is over 12, and not everyone is expected to verbally participate, you're highly likely to observe at least one person "nodding off." If you have to lead a meeting at this time of day, offset sleepiness with *Check In question* that encourage critical processing. If you are leading a meeting after 4pm, help people's brains harness natural boosts in out-of the-box thinking by selecting a questions that favors creativity.

Check In works in professional settings when a structured start is not already in place. Most meetings could benefit from one. Daily huddles are a form of check in, with the question assumed "report on what's essential for us all to know." Teams that huddle together frequently tend to catch more slip ups, offer support more quickly, and socialize more naturally[34]. This is all good for the bottom line and for our sense of fulfillment. Use one of the questions included here during a huddle to on a weekly basis to spice up the attention and engagement of your team and reduce the passivity that often comes with repetition.

Effective *Check In* leverages power of a typical beginning to advance group goals. Here are examples of when *Check In* works well.

✓ Start of Regularly scheduled meetings

- ✓ First on the agenda of a workshop, program, class, collaboration or group
- ✓ Daily huddles
- ✓ First Words of Strategic or Social Offsites
- ✓ Kick off community events
- ✓ Starting social get togethers and events or celebrations (try it at a wedding!)
- ✓ The onset of a shared meal
- ✓ Discovery calls with potential clients
- ✓ First part of consultation/coaching/medical appointments (instead of How are you?)
- ✓ Beginning of significant holidays or vacations

Non-traditional beginnings. Before we move on too quickly, let's look more closely at beginnings. We tend to think of beginning in a black and white manner. It's the start of, the first thing, or the opening of something. We look for structural or logistical beginnings and often miss the other psychological, social, or contextual ones.

Beginnings can be created at any time. They are naturally expected at the start of things, yes. But as a leader, sometimes you are called to manufacture a beginning where there isn't a clear-cut start or finish to something. Some of my favorite moments in my own life, and historically, are beginnings that are "in the middle" of something. For example, most of us feel the massive inspirational impact of Martin Luther King Jr's famous I Have a Dream Speech. One of the most beautiful parts of that story is left out--he never planned to talk about that dream on that day. That entire part of his speech was provoked through the support of a fellow congregant in the background who yelled "tell them about the dream, Martin!" and that's when Dr. King created a new beginning. I don't remember what preceded those lines. Most of us don't. What matters is, that at any point, we can, and are asked to, begin again.

Where can you begin again, right now, in your life?

A true icebreaker is something that creates a beginning in the middle of something else. I'm sure you're trying to avoid remembering all the times you've been forced to participate in an Ice Breaker or worse yet, you were told you had to lead one. Let me assure you: breaking the ice is a powerful skill.

The phrase comes from the men who had the responsibility to break the ice around a ship, so it could move ahead in spite of tenuous weather climates or conditions. Imagine that for a moment. The courage, the competency and the sheer force these men had to yield in order to safely do their jobs. The goal of their work to break down the most visible obstacle that prevented the ship to efficiently move forward. An icebreaker plays a powerful role.

It's wasn't necessary to break the ice at the beginning of the voyage, nor was it needed at the end. It was needed in the middle. True icebreakers belong in the middle of something, when unexpected "speed bumps" on a team emerge.

Check In is an easy to use discipline to *generate* a new beginning that gets us moving in the right direction. Here are some scenarios when it is likely a *Check In* would serve this desired outcome:

- ✓ When you sense there may be a misunderstanding, or possible upset/conflict present
- ✓ When decisions are being made without the input of key stakeholders or players
- ✓ When group conformity or biases are present
- ✓ When you need to highlight diversity or divergent thinking
- ✓ During a social get together that needs group cohesion
- ✓ During a strategic meeting or planning session where brainstorming is involved
- ✓ In a session or class or conversation that needs an immediate change of energy

When Not to Do a *Check In*

There are several times when *Check In* would be contraindicated. You wouldn't use a power saw outside in a rainstorm. Similarly, there are times when using this tool would not be helpful for the group. Be mindful of these times:

✓ After 8 pm. We are less capable of managing our emotions, our thoughts and our communication (nonverbals + words) later in the day. Research shows that this is a period of time when most people "say things they don't mean." Our biology and our brain often are geared to relax and power-down rather than perform. Try to avoid putting yourself and others in the position where they are blurting something in a tired, or often, vulnerable state of mind.

✓ Right after a previous *Check In*. This tends to make people rather impatient with the process and annoyed with the people asking them repeated questions, even if they are a new person. Just consider how many times we need to Check In while flying, when on a customer service call, or when visiting a health provider. The average person is usually stressed, annoyed or tired after going through multiple, similar check-points.

When you are tired, stressed or hungry. It is likely in these moments that you are going to not effectively use the tool, and you may hurt the trust of the team in the process.

Time doesn't have to drive our social experiences or our shared results. It shouldn't be defining our people either. But that doesn't mean that it needs to take a back seat and we all just need to "go with the flow." *Check In* should reorient our time together to serve our essential goals and priorities.

CHAPTER SIX

Who To *Check In?*

C **heck In** must be lead differently depending
on the people it is serving. It is designed to
be used *with* people, not on people.

We all have had experiences of people using
some newfound technique on us, not necessarily *for*
us.

Don't be that person!

If you've made it this far in reading the book, I'm
sure you are committed to serving others by using
Check In. To ensure that you are using it for and *with*
people, remember to explore your true
motivations, the physical and emotional context of
the group, as well as your choice of timing. Revisit
these parts of the process *before you start every
Check In.*

How you facilitate it will require subtle changes
depending on your audience. Here are the main
things you need to know to optimize a collaborative
dynamic and support your desired intention.

Consider generational dynamics. Here are some ways to use check ins with people of different ages.

- ✓ *Check In* can be used with people who are four years or older. For children under the age of twelve, make sure you repeat the directions a bit, and give gentle reminders to wait their turn. They are likely to surprise you how quickly they catch on.
- ✓ For adults over the age of sixty, make sure you acknowledge that this process might seem unnecessary, awkward or frivolous at first. People in this generation have had less exposure throughout their lifetime to thinking about their own thoughts/feelings compared to other generations. Some are likely to easily accept the process and others may need a little bit more coaching, explanation or plain old trail and error before they share authentically. Be mindful to accept where they are, and also to keep using the tool with them. It is likely they have a lot of wisdom to share, and will appreciate an outlet when they are led well by the facilitator.

Manage interaction styles. Here are some ways that consider people's varying levels of social energy exchange during interactions:

✓ People who identify themselves as clear extroverts tend to be more eager to *Check In* than others, even those who see themselves as extroverted, but not extremely so. If you have a group comprised mostly of extroverts, you will want to underscore that every person will be heard, so "manage how much you choose to share." You may need to say this a few times before the group dynamic shifts away from oversharing.

✓ People who identify themselves as clear introverts tend to be less eager to *Check In* than others, even those who see themselves as introverts, but "the social kind." If the group has more than seventy percent introverts, you may experience more quick, superficial responses and silence when first starting out. Facilitators (especially extroverted ones!) often think they've done something wrong if no one shares much, or the group seems very resistant to connect back to one another during the debrief. Fight the urge to give up the process or take this response personally. The more you model sharing your thoughts and feelings in a clear, concise, and yet revealing your personal

106 | KRYSTAL J. WHITE, PH.D.

truth, the more introverts will be inspired to
do the same. They have the same need for
connection as extroverts. They just need
more space in order to do so.
✓ Remind mixed groups that *Check In*
equalizes voices. It enables more quiet
members of the group to speak up, and the
more expressive ones to listen. Keep saying
this before using the tool, in the debrief, or
in reference to why you use it consistently.

Shift with group size. Shift your delivery and
manage your expectations as the group size alters.
Understand that:
✓ Groups of six to twelve people tend to
express the most amount of diversity,
reducing the tendency toward social
conformity or loafing. Numerous bodies of
research across social, evolutionary and
economical psychology suggest that size
does matter in terms of influencing
individual mindset and group behavior[41].

By yourself. Individual *Check Ins* require a lot of
discipline. Answering these questions on your own
is likely to provide you with some self-insight, but
we tend to move quickly when answering questions
for ourselves. We might spend a few minutes
pondering our answer, but the impact of saying it to
ourselves pales in comparison to saying to another

human being. The questions in this book are designed to catalyze impact through social expression. Although they can be used for individual reflection, their potential is maximized in communal response and listening. There are other resources available that are better designed for individual insight.

One on one. Using *Check Ins* with one other person can be either extremely easy or challenging. The polarity depends on how emotionally intelligent, open and willing each person is at the right time, in the right space. Make sure that the location and timing is optimized, and both people are in the right space to share at a deeper level.

Dyads are a bit tricky when it comes to using this tool. First, peeling back the superficial tendencies of our conversations is a LOT more noticeable when there is only one other person starting back at you. Second, power dynamics have a much more significant impact. Meaning, unless the culture has been trained to be transparent and genuinely truthful, and/or the follower has a high capacity for self-expression, there is a probability that some of the answers may be more for "show" and less for understanding and connection. Third, there is a normal flow of conversation each dyad tends to adopt early on in a relationship. It requires some amount of courage to impose a structured process and interrupt this flow. Doing so occasionally, however, is likely to lead to enhanced results. A significant group of my friends, colleagues and clients started to do a once a week/month/quarter *Check In* with their partner as a result of reading *The Letter Code.* They typically use *Check Ins* designed to amplify shared awareness of each other's needs for help, growth goals, complaints, gratitude or "more of" "less of" requests. All of them report that when they occasionally use a structured approach, that they feel more capable of connecting effectively.

Get some familiarity with the tool before using it one on one. Groups tend to be more forgiving and competent than dyad at following the guidelines.

If you're introducing it to a pre-existing relationship, acknowledge that the tool might feel a little awkward at first. Be sure to express that feeling this way is natural. You'll have to try it out a handful of time (not two times, but less than eight) to get the gist together.

Here are some tips for 1:1 *Check ins*

- ✓ Try it out with a group before you try it 1:1.
- ✓ Acknowledge it may be awkward at first
- ✓ Go first (unless the other person seems excited to answer)
- ✓ Select a Getting to Know you *Check In* if it's your first time doing it with this person. On repeated *Check Ins,* select questions aligned with your desired outcome.

Check In is strongly recommended at the start of routine meetings between a manager/supervisor and an employee. The manager should express that it may take a few trials to get the hang of the tool together, and that one of the intentions is to genuinely listen and understand the reality and perspectives of one another. Just using *Check In* effectively in this one situation is likely to reap significant benefits for positive affiliation and conflict reduction.

Check In with groups (3–14 people). This is the optimal group size to maximize the impact of *Check In*. This is where the power of the group is most felt. Effective facilitators not only are made aware of the group norms, beliefs, and needs, they also can shift them. The majority of this book is intended to be used with groups of this size. Follow the tips and suggestions throughout each chapter and you'll be set up for success.

This size of group is the best to practice using the tool as well. As stated before, typically in a group this size, there will be one individual whose presence helps enforce the guidelines or whom actively reminds others to follow them.

It is notable to mention that you can use *Check In* in social contexts with groups of this size as well. I have a reputation for leading it when guests are invited over to my house for dinner; we do a special version of *Check In* every year at Thanksgiving. In this more laid-back context, people's initial reactions to having a singular conversation a bit jolting. Many people are habituated to being/listening to "a conversation hog." They may expect the talk to stay superficial. Some possibly prefer the "going off in many directions" quality conversations at social gatherings tend to possess. When a facilitator steps in and "breaks the ice" of this dynamic, it can be a bit jolting.

Fight these initial reactions and facilitate a *Check In* despite the first impression. Be a more relaxed conveying the guidelines, and yet make it clear that people shouldn't interrupt or ask questions of others. The result, almost always, is one person expressing gratitude to listen or share a more genuinely. Most people enjoy getting to know who is in the same room with them beyond small talk and exchanging a few facts.

My good friends once had me over for dinner and their 5-year-old boy immediately pointed out their dinner *Check In* jar. On a twist of the normal guidelines, we each pulled a different question and took turns at the beginning of the meal giving our answer. For this extroverted young child, he practiced listening. For the adults, we practiced teaching ourselves to listen, too.

Check In with large groups (>14). Groups larger that contain more fourteen people require more energy to coordinate *Check In*. Social psychology and our own experience of being in groups this large tell us that as the number increases, so does

CHECK IN | 111

the amount of distraction, dissension, and loafing (e.g. expecting other people to initiate or respond). Individual responsibility decreases, as does individual expression. These are essential qualities we aim to increase with *Check In*.

When facilitated well with this group size, however, *Check In* has exponential results. It completely sets the tone for offsite trainings or conferences and workshops. It frequently opens the participants eyes open to the people around them and sets a tone for engagement and interaction at the very beginning. Plus, it gets people physically moving. This stimulates more mental energy and enthusiasm than is typical in most professional settings.

Here are some tips for large group *Check Ins*.

✓ Break people into groups of no more than three people to do *Check In* together. Ask the large group to "find two other people in the room and gather in groups of THREE people." Once the group has assembled (and not before!) then give the directions

✓ Reduce the debrief to only two comments from the large group about their experience. Then make a reference to your intention for the *Check In* and move ahead to the agenda.

✓ Expect a lot of chatter. Some groups won't follow the guidelines. Others will. This is normal, and is worth drawing to the group's attention. Some groups may need to "break the guidelines" a bit that day, and others may need to stay within the given structure. Both are ok, we just want them to be aware of it.

✓ Give the group six to eight minutes to complete their *Check In*. When there is about two minutes left, call that out (e.g. "You have 2 more minutes").

✓ Expect that some groups won't finish. Direct the group that if they didn't, to make a point to find the people who didn't have a turn and listen to their response. You are likely to see the groups regathering during break.

✓ This usually takes about ten to twelve minutes when done efficiently. It's perfect to follow it up with a short coffee break, allowing the group to socialize and reset for the rest of your time together.

I once led *Check In* with a group of over thirty employees who were gathered for a day long training. The initial *Check In* honed our attention on the learning to come, and for many, immediately reduced their anxiety for missing regular work. A few hours later, when I was directing them into groups and giving them a set amount of time together, I shouted out "what time is it?" When three people simultaneously responded in union "9:11" the room fell immediately silent. Indeed, the day was September 11th. Without having to say a word, more than 37 articulate, expressive professionals respected *minutes* of silence. That kind of shared listening is rare. *Check In* absolutely helped primed our group willingness to join together in that very special, respectful, and memorable moment.

No matter who you are doing *Check In* with, the results can be immediately felt, most noticeably to the facilitator and those who gave or heard a very real response. What makes this tool essential to the spirit of our communities, however, is the unforeseen impact it makes after it is completed. The real impact of the tool comes in those unplanned for, and uncoordinated moments, where the group is primed for sharing meaning and action.

Choice Is Always Available

We often don't know the questions we need to ask in order to receive the answers we need to hear.

That's one of the benefits this book offers—it asked you many key questions along the way. How many of them did you take the time to truthfully answer? .

It will offer you 52 more in the pages that follow. It is up to you if, how, when, where or with whom to use them.

You always have a choice to answer life's great questions. This is your internal, powerful birthright—life speaks through you. You choose what your life will say. Every *Check In* is a choice.

And every choice is a vote for the future you desire.

Here is one thing I know to be true—we need one another to learn about ourselves. We need one another to become better. Why, how, where, when and what we ask of one another will determine the quality of our relationships. Why, how, where, when and what we answer will determine the quality of our sole existence.

The time to work on this **is now**. We need partners, friends, bosses, children, politicians, advisors, artists, elders and consultants to get better at asking good questions. We don't need an Executive Shaman. We need you.

Check In is not a panacea for all our contemporary communication needs and issues. It is only one tool intended to help us communicate the truth of insightful citizenship. The master of *Check In* will have a competitive advantage over others who choose not to ask, and/or not to answer good questions.

 *"Never doubt that a small group of thoughtful, committed citizens can change the world; indeed, it's the only thing that ever has."*

Margaret Mead

This book gave you the why, the how, the where, then when and the who, and how of using *Check In*. Now, it's your turn. It's incumbent on you to actually do something with it. The time is upon us to discover our own truth, define our intentions and then deliver them compassionately to others.

Live your intentions out loud.

What will *you* choose to share?

I'm here with you. I Care. I'm listening.

52 QUESTIONS

1. What do you *really* do for a living?

2. If you could earn a salary doing any hobby, what would it be?

Why?

3. Tell us about a person who has significantly impacted you.

Describe how.

4. Share something that you like,
admire or appreciate about yourself.

Why?

5. Share a recent success you've had and what helped you achieve it.

6. What is something you possess that doesn't really belong to you?

Why do you still have it?

7. What deserves our attention and recognition?

Variant: replace *what* with *Who*

8. What can keep you up at night or prevent you from getting enough sleep?

9. Describe what being a friend really means to you.

10. What is holding you back right now?

11. What brings you joy and energy?

Why?

12. "We _____."

Finish the sentence.

13. Share something that we can do now that would help us have more fun.

Variant: Replace *have more fun* with *another positive outcome* (e.g. meet our goals, trust each other more, enjoy our vacation).

14. What is something you need to say soon?

What impact would this have?

15. What is something you think we all have in common?

16. Share something that you are
proud about.

Why?

17. What is it like to be you?

Variant: Replace *be you* with *work on this team* or *have this job.*

18. Share something you like to do when there are no outside expectations, demands or responsibilities placed on you.

19. What is your biggest headache right now?

Name one thing that would make it better.

20. Share something that you learned from your childhood that you still use today.

21. Describe the last time you felt inspired.

22. What is something that you are lucky in?

23. What's for dinner?

24. If you could know the truth about anything, what would it be?

What difference would this make?

25. If you had one extra hour today to do anything you wanted, how would you use it?

26. Share something you recently learned.

What difference does this make?

27. If we only did or talked about one thing today, what should it be?

Why?

28. Describe an experience that you want to have again.

29. What is something you don't want to regret 10 years from now?

What are you doing today to prevent that?

30. What do you think your power animal is?

Why?

31. What would you like to get out of our time together?

32. How do people sometimes bother you?

How could we tell if you were bothered?

Variant: Replace *bother* with *distract, confuse, annoy, or overwhelm.*

33. Share something you truly like
about the person to your left.

34. Share where you think we are losing energy, momentum, or an opportunity.

Variant: Replace *losing* with *gaining.*

35. What's something true now that wasn't true before?

What impact does this have?

36. What do you think could be a "game changer" for us?

How so?

37. Tell us about the last song you sang out loud.

Include the What, Where, When, With Whom & Why.

38. Show and tell us about an item that you brought with you today.

What does this mean to you?

39. Share something from pop culture that you regularly enjoy.

40. What is something about yourself that you'd like us all to know?

41. Describe the best team you have been on.

What made it the best team?

How does this impact you now?

42. What's new?

43. Where is your true home?

How does this impact your life today?

44. What is something you want the next generation to experience?

How does this influence you?

45. What do you think is really going on with (_____)?

Fill In the Blank.

46. What is your favorite element from the periodic table of elements?

Why?

47. Tell us something you think we don't already know.

48. What have you've been putting off for too long.

Why do you think that is?

49. What's your reputation or something you are known for?

What do you think about it?

50. Share something that you are not willing to work on, change or do differently right now.

Why?

51. Describe a hunch you have right now.

52. If you were in charge of [fill in the blank] for a day, what would be your number one priority?

Why?

1. Goleman, D. (1995). Emotional Intelligence: Why It Can Matter More Than IQ. Bantam Books.
2. Epley, N. & Whitchurch, E. (2008). Mirror, Mirror on the Wall: Enhancement in Self-Recognition. *Personality and Social Psychology Bulletin, 34(9):* 1159-70.
3. Dunning, D., Heath, C., & Suls, J. M. (2004). Flawed Self-Assessment: Implications for Health, Education, and the Workplace. *Psychological Science in the Public Interest, 5(3):* 69–106.
4. Epley, N. & Dunning, D. (2006). The Mixed Blessings of Self-Knowledge in Behavioral Prediction: Enhanced Discrimination but Exacerbated Bias. *Personality and Social Psychology Bulletin, 32(5):* 641-55.
5. Mehl, M., Vazire, S., Ramírez-Esparza, N., Slatcher, R., & Pennebaker,J. (2007). Are Women really more Talkative than Men? *Science, 317(5834):* 82.
6. Wansink, B. (2010). Mindless Eating: Why We Eat More Than We Think. Bantam Books.
7. Kahneman, D. (2011) Thinking Fast and Thinking Slow. Farrar, Straus, Grioux

8. Lehrer, J. (2009). How We Decide. Houghton, Mifflin, Harcourt.
9. Staddon, J. (2014). Death by Stop Sign. *Psychology Today.* Retrieved from: https://www.psychologytoday.com/us/blog/adaptive-behavior/201605/death-stop-sign
10. Packer, M., Evans, A., & Sawyer, R. (Eds.), *Reflections on the Learning Sciences* (pp. 191–209). Cambridge University Press.
11. Siegel, D. (2009). Mindsight: The New Science of Personal Transformation. Random House.
12. Burgess, L., Riddell, P., Fancourt, A. and Murayama, K. (2018), The Influence of Social Contagion Within Education: A Motivational Perspective. *Mind, Brain, and Education, 12,* 164-174.
13. Christakis, N. & Fowler, J. (2009). Connected: The Surprising Power of Our Social Networks and How They Shape Our Lives -- How Your Friends' Friends' Friends Affect Everything You Feel, Think, and Do. Little, Brown and Company
14. Weisul, K. (2011). Why Lazy Co-workers are Worse than You Think. Retrieved from: https://vandernest.co.za/index.php/contributions/articles/1-why-lazy-co-workers-are-worse-than-you-think

15. Kennedy, C. (2019). Transforming your Organizational Culture to Build a Great Team. Retrieved from: https://www.studereducation.com/transfor ming-your-organizational-culture-to-build-a-great-team/
16. Sorenson, S. & Garman, K (2013). How to Tackle U.S. Employees' Stagnating Engagement. Retrieved from: https://news.gallup.com/businessjournal/1 62953/tackle-employees-stagnating-engagement.aspx
17. Samson, D., Apperly, I. A., Braithwaite, J. J., Andrews, B. J., & Bodley Scott, S. E. (2010). Seeing it their Way: Evidence for Rapid and Involuntary Computation of What Other People See. *Journal of Experimental Psychology: Human Perception and Performance, 36(5)*: 1255–1266.
18. Furlanetto, T., Bertone, C., & Becchio, C. (2013). The Bilocated Mind: New Perspectives on Self-localization and Self-identification. *Frontiers in Human Neuroscience, 7*, 71.
19. Gallese, V. (2009). Mirror Neurons, Embodied Simulation, and the Neural Basis of Social Identification. *Psychoanalytic Dialogues, 19*:519–536.
20. Appelbaum, S.H., and Kamal, R. (2000). An Analysis of the Utilization and Effectiveness

of Non-financial Incentives in Small Business. *The Journal of Management Development, 19(9/10)*: 733–763.

21. Griego, O.V., Geroy, G.D., and Wright, P.C. (2000). Predictors of Learning Organizations: A Human Resource Development Practitioner's Perspective. *The Learning Organization: An International Journal, 7, 1:* 5–12.

22. Evans, R. (2001). The Human Side of School Change; Reform, Resistance, and the Real-life Problems of Innovation, San Francisco, CA: Jossey-Bass.

23. Brun, J. & Dugas, N. (2008). An Analysis of Employee Recognition: Perspectives on Human Resources Practices. *The International Journal of Human Resource Management, 19:*716-730.

24. Brun, J-P., Biron, C., Martel, J., and Hivers, H. (2003), L'e´valuation de la sante´ mentale au travail: une analyse des pratiques de gestion des ressources humaines, Montre´al: Institut de Recherche Robert-Sauve´ en sante´ et en se´curite´ du travail.

25. Asch, S. (1995). Opinions and Social Pressure. Retrieved from: https://www.panarchy.org/asch/social.pressure.1955.html

26. Wood, A. M., Linley, P. A., Maltby, J., Baliousis, M., & Joseph, S. (2008). The

Authentic Personality: A Theoretical and Empirical Conceptualization and the Development of the Authenticity Scale. *Journal of Counseling Psychology, 55(3)*, 385–399.

27. Rilling J1, Gutman D, Zeh T, Pagnoni G, Berns G, & Kilts C. (2002). A Neural Basis for Social Cognition. *Neuron, 35*, 395-405.

28. Driver, J., Tabares, A., Shapiro, A. F., & Gottman, J. M. (2012). Couple Interaction in Happy and Unhappy Marriages: Gottman Laboratory studies. In F. Walsh (Ed.), *Normal family processes: Growing diversity and complexity* (p. 57–77). The Guilford Press.

29. LaRosa, J. (2018). U.S. Personal Coaching Industry Tops $1 Billion, and Growing. Retrieved from: https://blog.marketresearch.com/us-personal-coaching-industry-tops-1-billion-and-growing

30. Hammond, C. (2013). Time Warped: Unlocking the Mysteries of Time Perception. Harper Perennial.

31. Pink, D. (2018). When: The Scientific Secrets of Perfect Timing. Penguin Random House.

32. Gladwell, M. (2005). Blink: The Power of Thinking without Thinking. Little, Brown and Company.

33. Bauer, T. N., & Erdogan, B. (2011). Organizational Socialization: The effective

Onboarding of New Employees. In S. Zedeck (Ed.), *APA handbooks in psychology®. APA handbook of industrial and organizational psychology, Vol. 3. Maintaining, expanding, and contracting the organization* (p. 51–64). American Psychological Association.

34. Sue Houck. (2004). What Works, Effective Tools & Case Studies to Improve Clinical Office Practice. HealthPress Publishing.

35. Newport, C. (2016). Deep Work: Rules for Focused Success in a Distracted World. (2016). Grand Central Publishing.

36. Sapolsky, R. (2017). Behave: The Biology of Humans at Our Best and Worst. Penguin.

37. Williams, L. & Bargh, J. (2008) Experiencing Physical Warmth Promotes Interpersonal Warmth. *Science. 322(5901)*, 606–607.

38. Manuel, L. (2017). The Book of Circles: Visualizing Spheres of Knowledge. Princeton Architectural Press.

Human influence is limitless. You can decide what and who influences you. The resources found in the endnote section, as well as these included here, intend to support you.

Joincheckin.com

Ensure you get ongoing *Check In* guidance. We provide handouts, stories, products, new questions, and advice to maximize your results.

I train teams to develop and sustain shared disciplines that optimize the wellbeing of people's emotions, the openness of their minds, and the prosocial impact of their actions. This book may not move you to invest in some form of local of team building. If it isn't ready yet, that is okay. On the other hand, if you are inspired and motivated to take the time out to *Check In*, this website will motivate you to begin and keep doing the work. Make sure you visit often to stay motivated and enjoy all the potential benefits *Check In* can achieve. Start today by taking the ***Check In* Challenge**!

Coaching and direct guidance is the fastest and most effective way to learn any behavioral skill. Take yourself or your team to the next level by bringing in house and remote trainings for Check In directly to your staff, community group, learning program or organization The training combines hands on group experiential learning, individual coaching, and skill assessment in real settings to ensure proficiency. Each person who graduates from the program will be ready, willing and eager to lead *Check In* and enjoy its results.

Theexecutiveshaman.com
Leadership is not a job you fill, it's a lifestyle you choose. That lifestyle requires deliberate practice, intention setting, social attention and faithful followership. Collaborate with other leaders to transform work from the inside out. We actively believe that the more emotional intelligence and courage we cultivate within ourselves and others, the healthier and happier the world would be. A process improvement plan will only take you so far to effectively influence the modern workforce. If you want to perform better as team or connect better as a group, you're going to need a context improvement plan as well. Aim to change people's the mindsets and culture change will follow..

We design and deliver in-house or remote mindful leadership programs, resiliency trainings and coaching services to your organization. Individuals also can join a remote class or live workshops that help them identify their truth, discern their intentions, communicate openly and authentically, and inspire others to do the same. We are always offering new ways to learn together, reduce our cognitive biases and unconscious self-interest, promote community, and address our toughest social challenges. Join the tribe to stay current with what's happening.

Thelettercode.com

When it comes to intimacy, you have motivations that are undiscovered, desires that are undeciphered, and needs that are unexpressed. What you really need in a romantic partnership may not be what you want on the surface. *The Letter Code* is an essential, easy to learn tool to decipher why you love the way you love. Start loving from your heart in a way that really works for you. Let's encourage our loved ones to do the same. Visit the website to explore resources not available in the book and remain updates on research and new products designed to improve our conscious connectivity.

The Executive Shaman Podcast

We encounter amazing leaders every day in our normal adult lives. Tune into The Executive Shaman Podcast to learn how they practically lead with integrity, wholeness and mindfulness. You never know what insight you may discover from the diverse co-hosts on the program. Every show demonstrates dynamic collaboration. Together, we examine concrete behaviors that are helpful or unhelpful for the topic at hand, and always offer tangible ways you can improve your thinking, feelings or behavior for the benefit of others.

These episodes are the most relevant to *Check In:*
#13: The Power of Reflection
#40: Asking Good Questions
#48: Leadership Ego
#60: Start to *Check In.*

Connect On Social Networks

LINKEDIN: linkedin.com/in/krystal-white-801179109
INSTAGRAM: instagram.com/drkrystalwhite

Recommended Websites

✓ Greatergood.berkeley.edu
This is an online science and lifestyle news platform delivered in an uplifting and approachable way. Visiting the site always leaves me feeling positive.

✓ edc.polyu.edu.hk/resources/free_riders.pdf

This article outlines a thoughtful way to address "free-riding," or social loafing. This dynamic occurs when one or more members of a group do not fairly contribute to shared tasks. This article is written for undergraduate professors, but offers insight into how groups function as well as practical guidance to manage their dynamics. A key take-away: "Don't assume that students know how to work in teams."

✓ https://www.mindsightinstitute.com
This is a comprehensive online platform offering resources regarding the science of mindfulness. They offer numerous applications for infusing and practicing mindfulness in every domain of life.

ACKNOWLEDGMENTS

I have deep respect for each person who ever did a *Check In* with me. Especially your first time, when you didn't really know what you were getting yourself into. You might have thought to yourself "We *all* have to answer?" or "I have no idea what I'm going to say" or "No way am I going to share a lot" or "I wish she would stop talking." Whatever you were thinking, you did it. I am in awe of your willingness and respect your skepticism as well. You are worthy of being acknowledged first.

Those I need to thank the *most* are the repeat visitors, those who did, or still do, *Check In* with me routinely. Your devotion deserves recognition. *Check In* lives through me as if it were my personal version of *Green Eggs and Ham:* We have done *Check In* on a plane, we have done it on a train. We have done it in a box, we have done it over lox. We have done it there, we have done it every where. You have joined me every time. Literally. Even when I'm sloppy in leading it, or edit the question out loud, or want to do it together *at the wrong time and/or place.* (I once lead *Check In* during a camping trip with strangers in Switzerland. Every one, even the dude that answered "Oatmeal," offered their truth.) In hindsight, my eagerness must have been tiring. Thank you for tolerating and encouraging my obsession/passion/dedication to this process. I sometimes wake up at night and think back on these experiences. I am humbled that you trusted me with your true voice. I am honored that you **also** held space for mine. When I remember these *Check Ins,* I immediately feel at home. Do you remember the silly one I made up from a line in that pop song? Do you recall the one where he came out of the closet? Some of you may not remember the magic that I do. Others of you won't ever forget a moment, where something was shared that changed our perspectives, together, forever. I'll be saying "Thank You" as long as I am alive for the sacredness of hearing you, and the holiness of speaking to you. Our tribe is one of clarity, compassion and courage.

For the ones who gifted me by leading a *Check In* for me, I thank you.

For the ones that checked in on me first, beating me to my own punch, I thank you.

For the ones that chose to start with me, stay with me, or come closer to me while I wrote out this book the winter and spring of 2020, in the middle of quarantine & COVID-19 2020, I thank you. I know I was a little more zealous for *Check Ins* during this special time. I know you were a *lot more tolerant* than I gave you credit for back then. I recognize your generosity right now. It won't be forgotten later.

Here is a truth (yes, this again): We never really know who is going to take *Check In* to the next level, and we never really can preplan how it will play out. Yet scientists, poets and prophets have all told us evolution works this same way. We progress gradually, slowly, until suddenly, we are a different creature altogether. We become a better species together.

Like all amazing tools, *Check In* didn't originate from a single source. I am certainly not its original designer. I do not know precisely where this practice started. Contrary to some beliefs, it's not typically used in therapeutic circles, or at least those I am aware of. Some group modalities may use a version of this tool, but nothing as simple, or structured as the one outlined here (again, to my knowledge). It was more widely used in organizational and social/professional development practices since the 1960s. Different forms of the process outlined here had many champions from previous generations of leaders devoted to personal and professional development. I acknowledge those who use it today, or pioneered it in the past.

The master of the "Aha Moment," Eddie Seashore, has influenced my behavior and mindset regarding group dynamics and radical acceptance more than any other leader of my time. I am positive she had a hand here. I never met her, and yet draw on her example every day. Eddie: I want to have a little more of your spirit in me when I finally grow up. I am grateful you are part of my lineage.

To my mentors, friends, and respectable guides who came before me in WEO (The Workforce Engagement Office) at Landstuhl Regional Medical Center, I bow to you. To the executives there that lead by their truths and through their hearts: I won't compromise for anything less in my professional life now.

To all the participants of SLP, Frontline and every unnamed initiative I was lucky to lead: I thank you. To those who dangerously grew, who shared their codes, who became my friends, who hired me, who partnered me, and who now are scattered around the globe: trust that if you call, I will answer. *I* follow *you*. Our connection continues to be a light on for me when it is dark within or confusing outside. Trust that our work isn't over. We are being asked to stand up for conscious community. I believe you want more of it.

To all of you who supported the physical manifestation of this book, thank you. I recognize the team's talent and heart. To Gus, thank you for crafting a cover that compels people to explore beyond their first impressions. To Najat, thank you for stitching everything together into a useable form. To Eva, beautiful illustrator. You translate my not quite clear ideas into images I want to keep looking at. They, too, are more than meets the eye.

To Stephanie, thank you for pulling it all together. I am truly grateful for our friendship, your competency in truth-telling and your standards of excellence, especially in the midst of an unprecedented, stressful season.

This book is a consequence of connectivity. We aren't just in it together, we are together.

Thank you, to you, still with me at the end. Because you are here, I want to be here. May we be there for each other. May we get better at it too.

You know who you are: Yes.

Dr. Krystal White, Ph.D., is a leadership psychologist who optimizes our collective mental agility, emotional intelligence, spiritual connectivity, and behavioral performance. She designs and delivers high-impact trainings that get groups to think more freely, care more openly, and serve more selflessly. For over a decade, Dr. White was a civil servant for the Department of the Army in the European theater. She has a PhD in clinical psychology and completed her fellowship at Madigan Army Medical Center. She holds a Master's of Christian Leadership from Fuller Theological Seminary, and a Master's in Mind, Brain and Education from Harvard University. Her consultation business and podcast, The Executive Shaman, enhances the prosocial, collaborative behaviors of everyday, powerful people.